Rimbaud,

An Unheard Cry

Paul Fearne

chipmunkapublishing
the mental health publisher

Paul Fearne

Published by
Chipmunkapublishing
United Kingdom

http://www.chipmunkapublishing.com

Copyright © 2019 Paul Fearne

ISBN   978-1-78382-469-4

Readers Note

I have purposely left some grammatical irregularities in the work to give it a fragmented feel.
In the history of literature, we have gone from structured harmony, rhythm and rhyme, to the fragmentation of the modernists.
But what next? Like all good dialectics, we now strive for synthesis of these two modes.
That is why I have left some irregularities in, and taken others out.
In such a manner, we can derive pleasure from structure and technique, but also pleasure from that which is dissonant and fragmented.
Please enjoy.

Paul Fearne

There are times to go, and times to stay. And in this Rimbaud, you have excelled. But what of the night? You are there, where we all want to be.

A child prodigy, like no other. The deep beyond has you now, but you live! Your renunciation has left its mark on a bitter world. But we must not stop.

'A Season in Hell', your finest work. We all suffer, but your suffering helps propel us to that misty climb that is the world we know. And here, life.

Verlaine, your heart. Your parting embrace a willow that has no steel. Your Africa, a place to let, for the adventure of amazing graceless wonder.

And now, the vision. An unheard symphony in steps that are no larger than yours, Rimbaud. And when you left it all behind, wonder, and a little silk.

Your early Latin, a confidant. A mist that dispels no sound. A prodigy, it was true. You won your awards, and then came to live the life.

What is that which you say from the grave? Hold on, there is still time. But when we live, we live with heart, and passion, and the moisture of the air doesn't bother us.

The poems you sent Verlaine upon your introduction to Paris must have surely left their mark. You had others too, equal in greatness.

You wanted the Parnassians, to be them, to join them, but your sound was too great. You shocked and appalled with equal fervour.

There are times in our lives, when we reflect upon you Rimbaud, and we are amazed. How could someone give up poetry all together at 21!

There is nothing like an old saying. And here, when we have your words at our breast, 'bon voyage'!

When Verlaine was drunk, and bought that pistol, and shot you through the wrist, there was no going back.

In Africa, after your great renunciation, you sold guns to a local king. Why does this not shock us?

When we live in you, and through you, we find peace. And that is not all. We come to know a greater yearning, a reaching abyss that saves as it unfolds.

How do we come to see you, when you are gone? We read, and we listen, and come to have light where there was none.

You left a pile of books at the printers, un-disseminated, that wasn't found until years later. The luck of things.

Coming forward, you are the spirit now of an age that has no ilk. Who has the answers? You do Rimbaud.

Listening for the stars, you have not reneged. You have found a logos to the telos, and here, a mighty sound.

You had a strict mother, but that is of no consequence. The daylight does not fade on the hearth.

Yours is the way of all things. The night, the day, the soundings and the sea. Be with me Rimbaud, and there will be an answer.

Come now, we must suffice all. Rimbaud, your need to be as one with the sky is not our feather. We love you, but why did you fly?

Because your flight contained your greatness. This much the bards have sung about. And here, there will be nothing left.

You suffered so much in Africa, but you saluted the dawn. You kept up the sight of your life, and had it transformed.

You left your mark on Paris, the home of the literary. You had no money, and lived the bohemian life, flittering here and there.

The clouds did not have a say in your life. They were too far, even for you.

Verlaine's wife Mathilde sought you to blame for all of his misgivings. But there was more to this relationship than that.

Rimbaud, you are the sun, the stretching of the constellations, you are the vector, and the might. Be what may, you are here.

What is left of us, after we read you Rimbaud? We have nothing that can be salvaged, and nothing that can be said.

The test is in the weave of things, and here Rimbaud, we love to sail.

You were an avid walker Rimbaud, and this held your pecuniary distress in good stead.

The fashioning of autumn leaves – Rimbaud, you were a visionary; to derange the senses, this was your motif.

The sense to be senseless. You are the farthing of the night, the traipsing through illimitable wastelands.

See what is in the mist, Rimbaud. See what is there, and tell us what you see. We will listen, and then have our say.

Do not believe in anything else Rimbaud. Do not believe, there is more to come, and more to be said

A kettle whistle in the morning. That will suffice for us to be content until the ravages of time have had their say, Rimbaud.

With Verlaine, you went to England, and taught yourselves English, even going to church services to learn the language. Even translating your own poems.

The weather in the winter. The weather in the field. What is that you say Rimbaud? You will never come.

Avast, adventurers, come. Rimbaud is waiting, on the tether of every side-glimpsed hope. Be now Rimbaud, be the one who sails.

Your relationship with Verlaine was a tumult. Your sexuality encapsulated the traumatic. But have no fear Rimbaud, you are there now.

The snow doesn't fall here, Rimbaud, it only hovers, and then lets itself rise. Why is this? Only you know the answer Rimbaud.

Come now, do not be pleasant. Be terse, and let the night reign like a fire that has no extinguishment.

A withering that has no vine. A masthead that feels no invective. Rimbaud, you sing, but your voice is only heard by the moat.

Here we say something that the world has no need of. The vastness of it all. Rimbaud, will you come?

You light us Rimbaud, with a fire that stills as it sears. There can be nothing more than this, in each step we take.

The seething remembrance is of you, Rimbaud. The density of the wire fills the void with all that can never be.

You knew, before you went to Africa that your work had adherents. And this much carried you away, the land of a thousand windows.

Gaining in momentum, your work now defies, and it seeks forward. Rimbaud you have won, as the night does not close in.

A switch, and then the end. Rimbaud, you have conquered life, and now, in your dotage, you can look back on things, and have them consolidated.

A well-spring, and then life. Rimbaud, you found a way, and not knowing, have conquered the sand between your toes.

You created worlds with your poetry, hallucinatory worlds, that sing as they breathe, and lapse as they come.

The distinctiveness of your prose poetry, echoes Baudelaire. And when in the midst of life we look, we are there. Never have the sands been so sure. Rimbaud, you are the one who fights, and your Africa, no flight.

The silence, the need, the overwhelming want. You are it Rimbaud, the tempting of all that is.

A catching that bears no harness. Rimbaud, your star shines. In the word, in the sound, despite what we have.

Rimbaud, a noise. It is not our noise, but the spheres, as they move around a tender world.

The catechism of all that is. Rimbaud, must I tell you once again, we are here, and we are waiting.

Clanging, I will not stand for it. We must see you in the in-between of things Rimbaud, and here do what we want.

A glass full to the brim. A much needed respite. And here Rimbaud, a chalice. Shall we drink?

Keeping still, so that the dawn will cast its rays. Rimbaud, you are the moon, as I am the sky. Verily.

The sense of it, we have the solace. Rimbaud, you came and went, and in this motion is everything.

The need is the want. The want is the need. You are free of both now Rimbaud, and we love you for it.

There was a time in your youth when you dreamed of respectability. But you could not have it. You were what you were.

Far from itself, your desire was a train, and your harbour a bridge. What is more, you came to be the source, and the noise that followed.

You are here now, where bridges do not dream. Your Drunken Boat nothing other than simplicity in otherness.

Hearing more, seeing less. This exposure was a tight enclosure. Be in us here, Rimbaud, and you will be more than enough.

Gaining in momentum, your corpus spreads, and you know not why. This is the way of all things, and you, Rimbaud, have captured it.

There is a sound I cannot explain. It is our sound Rimbaud, as we once again fight for those who are neither here nor there.

You once were interest in finding work in a box factory. This would have suited you, except that poetry was your vocation.

The diameter of the circle is life itself. The whirring we feel between our eyes is this distance. Rimbaud, did you ever love?

The feeling we have for the stars is your feeling Rimbaud. In it, we touch the infinite, and soar to that place that is always there.

There are classes for this, Rimbaud. How to be great. They are called biographies, and they teach the fire – that is your fire, Rimbaud!

Rimbaud, you are the tempest that reaches. You are the song that does not hear. You believe, as we all do, that flight is here for the taking.

What we say when we reach you Rimbaud, is not the salience of the drive, but of the small that dances within.

The things we wish for, are enough to save the weathering from more. Rimbaud, what you have done cannot be repeated.

There is nothing left in us Rimbaud. There is only the tempest as it blasts. But here, where the noise of the most derided sing, we find it.

The feeling, and the doing. Rimbaud, you must hark, and here leave a little breath, to dance amongst the embers of fate.

Gathering up the petals, we see you Rimbaud. You are here, before our unbelieving eyes.
Having the chance, I see it. But Rimbaud, you moan, and dispel the mist of all that is. We will be, and in being, win.

There is something more to be said here. There are chances, and all mighty winds. But we believe ourselves to be within reach, Rimbaud.

The discovery of a new way has us enthralled. But what do you say Rimbaud, before it is too late.

The now, Rimbaud, the now.

There is one chance, in amongst this, one chance to be like we never were. And here Rimbaud, the most ardent. The most soul engrossing.

The destiny of the fates. Be sure in your dealings, and fate will have you Rimbaud.

The dream is here. But what of the next? It is worthy of a summer's night Rimbaud.

Paul Fearne

Next to it, lies the need. Rimbaud you dealt with much. But this much more is true. The weight will lift from both of us.

The testing, and the strange. We have never thought so much, and to do so now, is more than we could have hoped.

The weather is here, Rimbaud. The way forward is in the mist. Can we risk again, when all that is left to risk is our hearts?

The tempest. It sings Rimbaud. It sings as if you never were in Africa. It sings as if the trains of our thoughts are derailed. It sings, yes.

What is the density of the air, that has you suspended Rimbaud? Is it in the foraging? Is it in the sand? Is it here, Rimbaud, with us?

The series of blows that comes is not of this world, Rimbaud. It is you, and now we, that have this insight. We must not tarry, but come!
The silence. We hear it. It is windy, and in need of salt. I will catch you, until all is lost. And then, no more of us, Rimbaud.

What play on words is this? What play do we disguise in winter gusts? It is here, the shedding of leaves. It is here Rimbaud.

The emptiness that cannot be contained. Rimbaud, I sense your unease. But what of the life we led. It is over, despite acceptances.

A rhythm that unities. A chance at happiness we just didn't take. Rimbaud, you mother was strict, but she knew, as we all now know.

The difference between things, is your domain Rimbaud. There comes a time when we must lift our weight, don't you think?

Come what may, Rimbaud. And here a silence that begs to differ. Be forthright, and escape the lion's clutches.

A well-spring, and then, you Rimbaud. There is never enough. There is always enough. And then, well, enough.

Gaining in on things. What is said in the starkness, Rimbaud, you can help with. Your goings, are our goings. Your need, ours.

What is this, Rimbaud? It is your lead, and your want. To be here, on the precipice of fate, is to be nowhere at all.

A falcon, in the wind. A falcon, that tarries long. What have we said Rimbaud, that does not sit aright? It is here, yes.

Gaining in momentum, the dreams of yore are distilled before our very eyes, Rimbaud. The dust, it settles, and then – release.

The gathering of rose petals. This is for you, Rimbaud. This is all we want of you, to be the gatherer of all that is.

The belief, it is in all of us. It is here, and there, and everywhere. Rimbaud, you are the stiff upper lip, that slides no sails to guide. Here.
The niceties of the wind are not so nice. But Rimbaud, would you really have us derange our senses? Of course!

The semblance of things unsaid. The semblance of the night. Rimbaud, you must not tarry, you must only wind your way there.

The context of the fight. Verlaine, you were there, what was said to Rimbaud? There is nothing left of us, only the gnawing at winter twilight.

Seeing more, and seeing less. I am the one to treasure, as you have done Rimbaud. I am the one who waits, and sees more than the time.

Catching up. So much is left in the wind. So much which says, yes to the dawn. Rimbaud, you cast us off, but not before too long!

The sentience of it all. What do we say Rimbaud when the night will no longer have us, and each window is shut?

There is never enough time. There is always enough time. In you Rimbaud we have the seeds of a larger turning, in you, Rimbaud.

The seething of the rocks. The seething of the remonstrations. Rimbaud, you dance, as I have danced. You sing, only because you have no other way.

The listening of the sky. What do you say, oh fearless one? Rimbaud, you could not catch a bowl of daffodils. But you have fought and won.

The licentiousness of the daylight hours. Rimbaud we need you to be a catching, as the sunlight is a withering. Be in store.

The likeness to the stars. Here, Rimbaud, there is nothing else to give. Here, where the light peaks through, we will find ourselves again.

The likeness to the stars. The likeness to all that is. I come and am forgiven, as you are Rimbaud. You are a myth – we are the marker.

The high and the low. The in-between, and the distance. Rimbaud you waver, as we say yes, and then go to that further shore.

The thing which binds us to the raft of medusa is the thing that binds you Rimbaud. You must not come, you always must come.

There is time, so much time. But when we find ourselves again, we find you, Rimbaud. And here we are happy, in a roundabout way.

The test is in the water. Is it clear? Do we drink it? Yes we do, whatever its colour. Rimbaud, you are the source, as we are the winter.

The racing in colours absolute. Rimbaud, what have you been, that allows so much to be. There is now time to follow, as there is time to lead.

I am nearing the chapel. I go in. But what do you say to this, oh great one? What do you say to my meanderings, save this.

The insistences of fate. Did you feel them Rimbaud? Did you feel their pull? Yes, I suspect, and that is what dragged you through.

The never ending ride. Rimbaud you have not seen the tale in the sharpest gull. You have only seen what you need, and that is good.

The hope that we all have. You have seen it too, and there, Rimbaud, you will be until it is all over.

The distance is here. The way forward is clear. When there was a song, it was for you Rimbaud. Come and play.

The deep beyond. It is you, Rimbaud. I hear your name bugled through the night. And when we stop, it is forever.

The seeming in-between of the song and the solstice. Rimbaud, you come, and we know you to be the one who listens.

The harrowing need. Rimbaud, we could have asked you, but we have no need. Be strong, that is in you Rimbaud.

The water, it comes. We have no doubt. But, Rimbaud, you are near, and yet far. You come for acceptances, and then are gone.

The leaving is in part the truth. The way we have nestled into fate is up to you Rimbaud. Do not be pleasant, it will not suit you.

The catching of the silence. Rimbaud, your dream, is our dream. Your noise is the noise of ages. Come, I beseech you.

What we believed to be true, but have now forgotten. Rimbaud, you are the namesake that has no fibre. To be, to see, to live.

The shallows of the stream. They come for you Rimbaud, but you are strong. To catch a glimpse of you, that is our dream.

The withstanding is here. Rimbaud you have written – this much is true. But do you fall on your own feet? Do you stall?

What we have been told, is that we will not bite. Rimbaud, your shall is half covered in the ancient wonder. Cover it all.

The tempest is not of our making. The tempest sees, but does not hear. In this Rimbaud we have one foot on the stairs to everywhere.

Forever, it is here. The clouds do not harvest, as the bees do not bring. I will have more of what we say Rimbaud, and then leave.

Now, and again, the listening we do to stave of fate is not something we should be engaged in. Rimbaud, we must give in, and go with fate!

The testing of the waters. It is here, Rimbaud. There is nothing greater than this. We swim, and are then taken. But what of it?

The seeming impossibility of it all. Rimbaud, in your youth, you were once there. But now, we have something more, something inconceivable to the rest.

The time we spent in our heydays, was time well spent. But here, Rimbaud, there is nothing more to do, than wait. Coming into the light. I see the shadows now, before we had even forgotten ourselves, Rimbaud. Be the one, and I will follow.

Hesitancy, it is here. There is a light, but it grows dimmer by the minute. Rimbaud, you can help. Tell me which way to go!

Holding on to truth. I salvage what it is I live on. But Rimbaud, there is something more. Something we must not shed, in terms of endearment.

The wishing, and the fate. Did you feel fate, Rimbaud? Did you feel it as a strong man might feel the wind. Yes, I believe.

The hope we have, is never enough. The feelings we have are here for us, Rimbaud. Be clever, and it will dawn on us like a new day.

The distance that doesn't matter. The temptation to shine.
What is greater than this, Rimbaud? I would say nothing.

The test – it is here. Rimbaud, did you ever encounter such
a thing? I hope you did, of course you did. There is much to
be said for fate.

The silence in the gloom. What is this thing that holds us
back? What is this thing Rimbaud that will not let us be
decisive?

The feelings we have for the dawn are now here. But what of
the cost Rimbaud? What of the motion in heavy seas?

There is a chance that we will make it – together Rimbaud,
you and I. There has never been a better time than now.

The case that holds a thousand dreams. We have it, but
there is something that holds us back form opening it
Rimbaud – what is it?

The wrenching from the sails, the leaning to and fro. What
have we thought but all that is, Rimbaud. What can we do,
but all?

I have heard a sound Rimbaud. It is the sound of the earth,
as it moves us to that deeper shore. It is the sound of you
and me.
Be the one who laughs Rimbaud. Be the one who travels the
distance, and knows not which road to take. This is what I
ask.

The tempest is a lonesome tune. It is where we find ourselves time and time again. But here, where the fulsome rest, I find you Rimbaud.

The nearness of the furthest shore. Time is short my friend, so let us dance that last dance, and have an earful.

The repartee of the muses is all we can muster. There is no time for the now, there is only time for the now Rimbaud.

What we have found is nothing other than all. But when we let go of it – what then? Will we saddle up to all of us, and see what happens.

The music I hear is your music Rimbaud. There is nothing left to give, and nothing short of everything to go by.

The dark is in the wind. The dark is your dark Rimbaud, and here where the nights are like embers, I will find you.

You were born above a bookstore, Rimbaud – and this fashioned every part of your existence.

Rimbaud, you have shocked us. Shocked us into an unbelieving state. But we will recover, and go onto create like never before.

The distance between our love and our fortitude. Rimbaud, this much is a truth, but what can we say of all that doesn't live?

I sense now, an opening. It is you Rimbaud, as we come by new well-wishes, and new ways to be. Be the one who laughs Rimbaud, yes.

The simplicity of this star next to its companion. Rimbaud, you haven't lost, you have won, just as we have all have won.

What do we see when we are there? And where is there, Rimbaud? There is where the heart is. There is where our heart now is.

The final countdown. Rimbaud, we have made it you and I. We are at that simple place where the arrows of time point backwards instead of forwards.

You were brought forward one year at school for an amazing piece of prose history. Well done.

What have you done, Rimbaud? You have left us with no room to move. But that is alright, we are willing.

The further shore. Rimbaud, you are there, but where are we? We are coming close, but it is not in our step to falter.

The raining of daffodils. This much we see from our vantage. But what is in the afternoon between times? It is what we think.

I see you now, Rimbaud. It is as if you were a stallion, that has no recourse to the stars. I hear more in you Rimbaud than you could ever want.

Paul Fearne

The life we lead, is one of the solstice, and here, where we gain ourselves anew Rimbaud, there is time to become again.

The weather over ice. It is cold Rimbaud. But it is also hot. And here, where we gather ourselves anew, we will find solace.

The tempest is a bark that steels as it embraces. But what is more, my Rimbaud, is that withstanding is a virtue.

What I see, is neither near nor far. It is you Rimbaud, as you dive. As you dive into that full embrace that is time.

The clattering of footsteps on sandstone. We relinquish our right to be Rimbaud, and here, where the dance is slow, we will be slow.

The feather in the cap. This much is assured. But what do we have left, but all that is, and all that can be?

The right way to go. I am listless, and tired. We will not be with you again my Rimbaud, this is assured.

A nicety in the sand. This much has strength. And when I follow, Rimbaud, I will only follow for you.

The trees do not waver here. The trees only waver when we are not looking Rimbaud. Be not clever, it will not suit you.

The feeling we had amongst the trees is not here now. It is lost and gone. But what is that? Fear not, it is love, Rimbaud.

In one school year, you carried off eight first prizes. You were the prodigy of prodigies.

You used to write homework for your fellow students for a fee!

Rimbaud, you are the blast and the invective. You are what keeps us stirring in a heart that beats no more.

The silence we hear is your silence Rimbaud. And now, when we look, a small feather has landed just to remind us of you.

At school, you never blotted your paper. In you, there were no errors, Rimbaud.

What I say to you, Rimbaud, is this. You have never been so close to the sun as you are now. This is truth, and truth be told.

The diameter of the eclipse which burns our eyes is your diameter Rimbaud.

The sense we have that time will stop for us, is your sense Rimbaud. Time is never an eagle, and always a feeling deep inside.

You sent off a poem to 'Le Parnasse contemporian', the leading publication of the day, and lied about your age. You were rejected Rimbaud, but not from life.

There are poisons we should not drink, Rimbaud. But you have drunk them, and your Verlaine has too.

The merriment of the clouds is ours, Rimbaud. There are distances that know no might. There are times for changing, which are here.

The fire that burns, Rimbaud. The fire that troubles itself into motion, is here with us. Yes.

There are more times for crying that we ever thought. And when we dust you off, Rimbaud, here you flourish.

The tempest, it is aghast, Rimbaud. There are chances at life, but this we know. Only suffering can get us there.

The moisture in the farthing space. And when we think, we think of you Rimbaud, and come to that deeper point.

It is a testament to the daylight that living and breathing create a space that is yours to encounter, Rimbaud.

In your youth, you copied out a poem by Sully-Prudhomme, made some changes, and passed the poem off as your own!

Tell me about your mother, Rimbaud. She was hard on you, but did she make you great? I think she did, that is no mistake.

The following of the nuances of fate. Rimbaud, you are the wind. Rimbaud, you are the strength, as we are your disciples.

The nearness of the afternoon sun. Rimbaud, have you found your hand to play with the debris? Yes and no.

The fast and the dead. You were nearly dead by Verlaine's hand, but that is nothing to be worried about, is it?

The solstice is not a wind. The solstice is the wind. What do you think Rimbaud? Are you in or out?

The catching of the great. You achieved it Rimbaud, but yours was not a simple thing, but it never is.

Your mother wrote a letter to one of your teachers scolding him for giving you a copy of Les Miserable, advising against its subversive nature.

Now, I see you, Rimbaud. I see your course as the tributary. I know of no other way, than across, and down. Is this your journey also?

I am the one who sighs. And yes, Rimbaud, I hear your sighs also. And here, I have no rest. There is nothing that can be done.

The vacancy of youth. Even in your youth, you were trouble, Rimbaud. But that does not disturb us.

Coming back from the dead. You have done it a thousand times Rimbaud. But your life is not one of protest, at least in spirit.

The daggers of the heart. We see them, and judge them as we see fit. And Rimbaud, there can be nothing more.

A pit, a fragrance, the delight, and the perceptual. I am one to see, as I have no feet left. What is left, is for you Rimbaud.

Accentuated rhythms, that is what I see in you, Rimbaud. I see all the walking as a guide of things to come.

What is left? There is nothing, but this.

Rimbaud, you come for water, and have salt as your meal. But this does not concern us, for we ride together, Rimbaud, you and I.

The seeming trench of it. We know our lives to be a station that is in the middle of nowhere. But that is fine, Rimbaud.

Come and be a part of the grand adventure, Rimbaud. Come and see what is in store for us. It will be palpable.

The testament to this is written in all the annals of all the journals that have ever published a jot.

The catching of rays of sunlight. There is a nuance here, one that defies description, Rimbaud.

Holding on fast Rimbaud. There are times we must not see it, but there are times we must.

The mist, it envelopes. The times, they change. Rimbaud, you have left a legacy, that much has touched us, yes.

And now, the length. And now the time. And when we are through, rose petals, that have a sense of what is next. Yes, Rimbaud.

I tell you, before too long, that we are here to charge our glasses. You and I Rimbaud, we sit, and are forgiven.

The wasteland is ours, Rimbaud. It comes in spits and spurts, it has the here as the now, and when we come again, it will not be too late.

The farthing and the trumpet. They are close together, and as I said before Rimbaud, we must not wait.

The tempest. Why does it fascinate us? Because of its strength, Rimbaud. Its strength to test the very fibres of us all.

Rimbaud, we are here, the both of us. We are here to test the waters, and know that which is impossible to be possible.

A catching, that lets go the saving. Rimbaud, I will embrace you, and know you to be a friend. This much is for certain.

The seething of the rift. You were arrested on your first trip to Paris, for not having a valid ticket on the train, no money, and unable to give an address in Paris.

The sign post is clear. There is never anything but this. Never anything but the life we lead, again and again and again, Rimbaud.

The heart, it speaks Rimbaud.

Why, 'An Unheard Cry'?

This is the spark and the want. This is the need and the transposing. Rimbaud, you have life, as we all do, until the end. The end of what?

Coming into mystery, there are myriads who do not venture. And here where we live, there are more times than ever, Rimbaud.

The vagabond, and the twilight. We are here, my friend. You are the desire I seek, Rimbaud. Is this enough? Yes it is.

The dream, it lives, it barks, and has solemn rites. Rimbaud, you could accompany me. Yes you could.

The timidity of the trope. Be a well-spring in a place with no water, Rimbaud. Be us, and we will be you. Come and take on the foundry.

The last vestige. That much I say to you, Rimbaud.

And when the blades of grass no longer distil our footprints, there will be time to gather things anew, Rimbaud. Yes.

The summer heat, the winter's blaze. I have now, Rimbaud, a way to be free. And I will come for it in depths of night.

The hearing of the vine. Here we love, and here we die. And now, Rimbaud, a sense for the senseless. A time for the needy.

The very thing that bites, Rimbaud, is the very thing that saves. We are all saved in the end, but what of it. We must push on.

The vagrancy of the light. What we say is in the middle of all that is. This truth burns in you, Rimbaud.

What is there left, Rimbaud? What is there to do, but carry ourselves forward, and come into what awaits?

The forest awaits us, Rimbaud. The forest, as deep as a gorge, as long as a side-ways glimpse.

The happenings of the daylight. Be here, Rimbaud, I implore you. Be here, and never more.

This is the sky, Rimbaud, this is what it is like. The sky, and all she breathes.

What have the clouds to say, Rimbaud? What is it they wish to say?

And now, a wish. A wish to be covered in gold, and then relaxed, to times of ease, Rimbaud.

The wantings of dragon flies. They have in mind only what we have thought, Rimbaud.

There is in us more to say, Rimbaud. There is in us a feeling like the twilight, that has no recourse to the horizon.

And here, in the afterglow, a new need. Rimbaud, you have gathered for us a harvest of rich perfume that does not sleep, only for you.

What have we said, but that which does not speak, Rimbaud. And now the afterglow, as it winds itself towards time.

The catch in the seam of things. There will be more time than we ever had hoped. And here, we will sing, Rimbaud.

The last vestige of our cry. The last sense we have to be. And here, Rimbaud, a new belonging that gives us what we need.

And now, when we finally see straight ahead, a little bit of respite as we read you Rimbaud, and know you to be a missive that does not miss.

A camaraderie that speaks your name, Rimbaud. It is a friendship woven in silk, and has nothing left to give but itself.

A light across the page, this much I see in you Rimbaud. You are illuminated, as it were, and now you live.

I beseech you Rimbaud – do not falter. It is not in you, I am sure. But here, where we sing, a new life.

Rimbaud, you are treasured. Your cry is not unheard. Be the things we want, and I will be with you.

I have seen, in my wanderings, many things. I have heard, many things. But Rimbaud, you are the mist. You simply are.

Once upon a time, in a fairy tale, I saw you Rimbaud. I was there for your life. I did not mean to pry, but you have, indeed.

The difference between the gull and the eagle is no difference. And here, Rimbaud, you fly, and are forgiven.

Be the tune, be the sceptre of the night, be whatever it is that holds you back, but do not simply be.

There are chances that do not sing, and there are chances that do sing. And here where we love, Rimbaud, I will find you.

The direct engagement with the now, is your incalculable deliverance Rimbaud. Be forever now, and then, well, be.

The night is a rough. The daylight is more than we could have hoped. With sand between our toes, Rimbaud, we carry on, into what awaits.

When we have found a way, there is no more. When we commission the stars, they give up their translucency. Here Rimbaud, I find you.

The distance between the sea and the horizon is not one that can be measured. Here Rimbaud, we find the noise to keep us straight.

Beginning again.

And when we talk, there is only a small noise. We have found, in the in-between of things, a semblance of our former selves, Rimbaud.

What I do, despite myself, is to carry the windings of fate on my shoulders. And when this mighty work is done, you, Rimbaud.

The textual niceties and the fact are the campaign. And now that we have seen what will happen – onwards Rimbaud.

What is less, is in the middle. What is more, is at the very top. I have changed to be in the opposite. And here Rimbaud, you are with me.

The worrying of a thousand nights is in the meadow. Rimbaud, will you come? Will you come, and wipe the tears from my eyes.

The final course is here. There are no more trials, no more that cannot be done. Rimbaud, I sense your fear. But come. Come.

The withering of the lance. I hear you, but that is not a course. I hear you, but there is never anything more. Rimbaud.

This is the way. I have found it. I have found a way to create. But Rimbaud, so did you. On your many walking adventures, to be sure.

What is the life we lead? Is it a vapour in the sky? Is it a vacuum at the bottom of it all? Yes and no. Rimbaud.

I hear your cry, Rimbaud.

The white of the solstice. And then…

There are times that we find to our liking, Rimbaud, and times not. And there are times when we sing, and times when we sigh. Let us sigh.

The distance between the meadow and the raison hill is like a future we had forgotten, but now remembered, Rimbaud.

The following of likenesses in the breeze. We come for all that is, and leave with nothing other, than, well….

The gate to the cemetery is closed, for the time being at least. And here Rimbaud, the numbers are like silken ash. Never to be liked, always to be liked.

The rainbow that has no fear goes straight up, don't you know? And here Rimbaud, the triangulation of the night sky moves through us.

Forests and gagging might, I love you Rimbaud, as an arrow that has no name on it. What is here, is nowhere. What is there, cannot fight.

The little bit of calm, is in the wind. The little bit of solace is now and in there, gone to the graces.

The last of it that cannot be told to come to any master of any fate, and any troubadour of any missing piece. Yes Rimbaud. Yes.

The wishing and the ring, the solitariness and the conceit. And here Rimbaud, another chance at what is never believed

I am not here, as I am over there, as I cling to the mast head, during an amazing storm, and know not when to let go, Rimbaud!

The heart felt, and the new need. What is there more, that has neither the sense to be, nor the nonsense to love? Rimbaud.

Withering in case of attack. Having more than an outrageous sense of worth, that keeps us on guard, and has no newness to vent.

Rimbaud, instead of thee, I address the fates. But no, upon reflection I address you both, and have my rest here.

Closing in at speed, the carriage driver lets go of his controls, and the horses spill their weight as the rain spills her rapidity. Yes Rimbaud!

The little we have left is not enough to stop us, neither here, nor there, nor everywhere we look. Yes Rimbaud I will find you.
The mist, the time, the willow, and you, Rimbaud. Here we have our say, and it is not of the ilk we have wanted.

The child comes, and then we are beseeched. And now, a new song, that forever envelops, and knows a treaty well, Rimbaud.

The last of the fragrances that distil. Distil what? Distil everything into every other thing. This much is true, Rimbaud.

The nuance of the twilight, that lives and breathes, with a deeper breath. And here, the solemn rite of a today with you, Rimbaud.

Catching the ilk of the times. And here, where the never ending departs off every platform, except one, there will be time to conquer, Rimbaud.

You are the selling point Rimbaud. Yours is the life, as I am the vicissitudes. You are the life, as I am yours.

Catch and run. Catch and run. Be a mover and a come-lately, Rimbaud, and all that will be yours (as it already is!)

The mismatch of each feeling is ours to enjoy, Rimbaud. Do we ever make errors here – yes and no. There are times to be, and times to signal.

The tether and the cost. The love, and the about face, the time, and all that shall be, Rimbaud. Yes, we will come again.

What has forsaken us? What is there left to do, Rimbaud? There is more than enough talk, that is for sure.

The tantrum of the night. Be a galloping steer Rimbaud, and you will rule all. Be that which may, and you may indeed, yes!

A golden chime. A thing which eases. A thing which has as itself its remembrance. Here we stand Rimbaud, like all before.

What is the wishing away of? What is the wishing together of? What do we say when we see clarity? Yes, and then the waves Rimbaud.
The fire and the eyes. The next instalment, and the burning of the tethers, Rimbaud. I come for you, and know you to be in the thick of it.

Coming again, in harvest as in grain. Rimbaud, you are never far from the acceptance of things. You are never far.

 On one of your trips to Paris, you lived the homeless life, sleeping on coal barges, and scraping for food.

The most dreary incumbency is upon the ground on which we walk. And here, Rimbaud, we walk that stronger walk that is for us only.

Testing the shallow water for depth. There are sounds which
come, which should not come Rimbaud. But we hear them,
nevertheless.

Gnashing and Gnawing, gaining, and restraining. What is left
of us, my friend? We are here, but where are you?

A rhythm that wanders. And wanders the way of all things.
Be a sense of the old, Rimbaud, and I will come for you.
Yes.

Catching the slightest nuances of a word. An old saying
Rimbaud – where did it come from? What does it mean?
Nuances. Yes.

Having the sense to just do as you most feel, and relinquish
what is less than enough. Rimbaud, I come.

Rimbaud, you were most likely in Paris during the commune.
What did you see, where did you go?!

The water here leaves one foolish. Rimbaud, you are the
key, as you are the key hole. What do we say, when all is
lost?

Distances that bind. Well-springs that do not give water.
What we have is the all encompassing. Yes, Rimbaud. Yes.

Come and be my companion on this long journey, Rimbaud.
It is long and hard, and we may never make it back. But
come. But come.
Snaking through the vapour trail of our lives. This journey is
said to take all, but we will take it, Rimbaud – this much I
know.

The pleasure of words. The pleasure of the place that takes you, and the places they leave you to. Rimbaud, we will shine!

Have a semblance of vicissitude, and your goal is reached. Have that which is freedom, and all will be yours, Rimbaud.

The taste of the next. The sense that we will make it in the end. And here, where we are hermits, we will lead the most miraculous lives, Rimbaud.

The sense we have to stay, is here. The sense we have to be, is here. Rimbaud, are you the one who weeps? I suspect so.

The mistiness of it all, yes. Rimbaud, I come for you, and when you least expect, I give you heart to carry on.

The well-oiled machine that is in the nowhere. I hear you Rimbaud, but before you go, a new need, and a new want.

The fountain, that spills no water. The rose bush, that has no thorns. And here, I love the sound of longing, as it takes us both, Rimbaud.

I have never seen this, this splendour, this dilapidated incarnation. Rimbaud, will you come with me? To the middle of things, to the beyond?

Here is a life. Here is a saying. There was once a man… Rimbaud, do you have the dream still burning? Yes, then come.

Having sent for the coachman... Rimbaud, did you send for
him already? If you have, if you haven't, it matters little.

Rimbaud, are you there? Are you there, or here, or who
knows where? Yes I have found you, yes I have.

The cutting up of old paper. There is never a finer ritual that
dispels all that has come to pass, Rimbaud.
The telling of the speech of things. And here, where we
come for more of the same, there is a knee that has no
more, Rimbaud.

The sirens melody. Do we hear it, yes we do Rimbaud! It is
heard like the never before heard song of forever. Are we
strapped to the mast – yes!

Then come and be a story. There are wantings, Rimbaud,
wantings to change us into something we are not. Are they
here? – yes and no.

There are times that do not change us. There are times that
do change us. And here, Rimbaud, we both sit, and watch
for both!

A further shore. And here, Rimbaud, we sit and listen for that
little bit of silence that has been promised for us. This much
we can be thankful for.

The charging of winter glasses, the testing of underground
waters. And here Rimbaud, the fading of light, and all that
will come to pass.

The next thing to do, Rimbaud. We have come this far with what we have, and now we will have both!

The listening we do to stave off time. The all-encompassing listening Rimbaud. And here, where we sing for the last time, a ferry that will take us there.

The sky is lit in such golden hues, I do not know what to say, Rimbaud. I am lost for language, as silk is lost for decay.

The hope we have that we can make it. Whatever our goals, Rimbaud, we can do it with a scope for the distance.

Ahhh, the tender and the hoping of fate. Why does she not stay? Because nobody stays, because only the mighty truly stay.

Kinship, and the revelries of the night. There are more turns in us that we ever thought possible. Rimbaud, we will come.

The mirror to our lives is more than we could have hoped. The mirror, and the life. The mirror, and all that is Rimbaud.

What is it, Rimbaud? Are you filled with the tempest, and cannot let go. Do be kind, and stay the round. This much I ask.

In the season, there is the rust. In the season, there is you Rimbaud. But do not be afraid, there will be more to come.

Sanctioning the roadway is enough to spill you Rimbaud. But it is not enough for me. You see, I have the flight of the gull in me. Yes.

In the little we see of each other, the more I become like my older self, in the trampling and the growing. Hear me now Rimbaud, I beseech thee.

The catching of finery. The toast, and the absolution. Here Rimbaud, I find you. You have gone to him who is never enough.

The withering on the vine. The time it takes. And when we come through, there will be times to rebuke, and times to dwell. Be kind Rimbaud.

And now, Rimbaud, the start of something magical. And that is life in all her victories, and all her finery. Yes, a new start, Yes.

The story of the clouds is very near. Is it here, Rimbaud? Is it where we want ourselves to be? And then some.

Come Rimbaud, we must all be seers, in your grand tradition. But what would be left of us? Not much.

The dream, the overriding wash, that harbours more than he brings. And here Rimbaud, a sense that life can take us there. But where?

Coming closer than ever before. What is left of the fog, Rimbaud? What is left of our ease? What is left?

The camaraderie of fate. Listen Rimbaud, I will tell you a story. It is not of this world. It sings as we do, but not in perfect pitch. It sings!
Come and applaud the meagre man, his is of the earth. He is of the trail and the Whitsunday wedding, born to be sure.

The tiring of the net. It brings so much, but has lost its way. Why is that? We do not know. We only beg to differ.

The listing of the seas. They do this for a reason. But we do not know what it is that makes them so. Rimbaud, come.

The seething. The mass. The intrepid sailor, who finds no rest. There are things here that do not guide, but only take, and in taking Rimbaud, diminish.

This is the start. This is the starting point of so much. I have a plan, and it stays with me, through it all. Rimbaud, can you see it?

The distance. The library. The wanting. The canary. All the more reason to see it through Rimbaud. Yes, let us see it through!

The hope. The hopeless. The tether. The utmost. Where do we find ourselves, Rimbaud, where do we see ourselves going?

The tide. The newness. What is it for this life of ours? Why do we strive, Rimbaud, when all that is made is made of milk.

The hope of the now. This is where we are, Rimbaud. We cannot escape it. But do not wander, we will be fine, we hope!

The hapless and the true. And here Rimbaud, a mighty feat is achieved, right before our unbelieving eyes!

Some of your early poetry, Rimbaud, was lost for lack of a stamp!

Here we go then!

The seething that we have of you Rimbaud, is a trial. A trial of magnanimous sculptures.

There is no time.

There is the time we have remaining – but what is this Rimbaud?

A sense, and then the senseless.

We are last, but we are endless.

We come for you, Rimbaud – and have our hearts full.

Do not dream in this place, there is nothing left Rimbaud.

The sepulchre is empty.

Why do we have no wind, when our sails are full blown,
Rimbaud?

The distance in the miniature of things, Rimbaud.

There are times when we must look, and times not so.

The fundamentals are alight, and nothing can put them out.

What the fire has in its sights.

Rimbaud, there is but the briefest of times. And here, where
we falter a thousand times, something new, and as yet,
unheard.

What can be said, is not unsaid. What can be life, is not
what is in the distance. Rimbaud, we will carry you, as they
carried you in Africa during your final days.

The whispering of trees in final distance.

The rhythm and the cadence. Here, where angels have their
way, there is more to say.

The furrow on the brow of greatness.

The mis-interpretation of reality.

What we thought was a prelude, but is nothing more than a
syncopated absolving.

Rimbaud, a new need.

Rimbaud, an old need.

The testing of the temperature. Rimbaud.

The newness of a fading breath. Yes Rimbaud, it is you.

The way things are. Yes Rimbaud, we have come.

The smile on the eyes of forever.

The beyond, the depth of it – a shock.

Rimbaud, we let go, and have the ride of our lives.

Do not be afraid. Rimbaud is here.

The dreaming that has sent us here.

Rimbaud, can we dance with you?

A hop and a step, and then the remainder.

Catching sight of all.

What is in the way? Nothing. What has been seen, but all. Rimbaud, there are times to be, and times to not linger.

The little bit of acceptance. It is in the arc of things Rimbaud. It is in the arc of things. This much is assured.

The little bit of respite we take with us is enough to feed the further shore. Rimbaud, can you not hear me – you are gone!

The magnanimity of it all. And here, where we sing, the lasting feathers of this place are laid bare. Yes, Rimbaud.

I am tired, like us all. I am tired of the wind, the rain and the hail. But then I look again, and I love it – there is rain Rimbaud!

The feeling I have for you Rimbaud is like a moon that has no visage. No hat to soak in times of dryness.

The forest knows only truth. The forest knows the time of things. Rimbaud, you are last, but I will come again for you.

And now, the distance.

The night time. The weathering of winter storm on parched earth. Rimbaud, there are times in all of us. Times to pray, and times to rescind.

The foraging we all do in this life, is more than we had hoped for. Rimbaud, you are the wind as we are the sails. Hear me, oh Rimbaud.

The newness of a fading sun. The placating of nerves of wonder. Rimbaud, there is time.

What must we say, when we hear? We must say yes, and keep going despite the rag tide blues that jingle in the air.

The hegemonic and the gaining of grace. Rimbaud, I hear your cry, as we all have, and know it to be one of no end.

The feelings of the day. They come, as we all come Rimbaud, as we all saddle up to the breeze, and have it more than ever.

Watching, and waiting. Waiting and watching. And here, where landfall is a gift, we will know ourselves, Rimbaud, to be alive!

The climate never changes here. Hot, and with no respite. But you Rimbaud, have changed it, and for this, we are thankful.

The wishing and the receiving. What comes, comes, and what is here to stay does not languish. Rimbaud, your star.

The feeling I have for the noise of life does not diminish. And here, where we are left to wander, there is a spark that knows no breath, Rimbaud.

The sentience and the dream. They are coupled, in aeons and in sounds. Rimbaud, come and wander with us.

The never ending bark. She is here, Rimbaud, here in reams of light. Be the tempest, and the dream will have you.

There can only be a truism here. And only because the dance is one of side-ways movement. Be the thing that comes, Rimbaud.

Increasing in size, the silence at the cusp is like a new found longing that says of itself, I am new – I knew!

The fire is lit, there can be no stopping it. No reason to be, no life to submit. Be the thing that harbours, and all is yours Rimbaud.

The withering is without. Without rhyme or reason. Rimbaud, you have rhyme, and your reason was yours.

What can be said of this, that has not already been said? Here, Rimbaud, you come, until there is no forest left.

What is authorial intention? Is it the mist, or the song, or you Rimbaud? Is it the trees, or their lack. It is you Rimbaud!

Stepping on unfamiliar ground. We step, and then are here. Rimbaud, we step for you, and know no other way.

Having what is best. Knowing what is worthwhile. We sing, and further ourselves unto the chime that does not register, Rimbaud.

A glimpse, and then…well everything. I will find you in the tavern, and know you to be strong, Rimbaud.

What is left of us at the end – well everything we need, and nothing else.

The seething, and the mass. Here, Rimbaud, the night does not cover us. The night, and all that rings true in our ears.

The gaining in moisture. What is left of us, here, Rimbaud, is nothing that we can speak of. I will come for you, and know you to be a trace.

Forever alive through your corpus, you sing and then are relieved. Rimbaud, I cannot find you. Rimbaud.

The mist – it comes. The mist, it envelopes you Rimbaud. You are unseen, but you are heard.

The need is in the hills. The want is in the daylight. My daylight hears no sound, but this is perhaps all we are.

The tempest is here Rimbaud. It comes and does not diminish. There are lights that guide us, but in the noon-tide, they flee.

The sentience of the horizon. It is like a new found babe, always rising, always challenging, never fleeing.

The distance of our own insistence. I see you, and know you to be more than we had hoped. Be the want, it is yours.

The stars, they have a sound. All we must do is listen, and the right way will appear, Rimbaud. Come to us.

In the middle of it, where is the destination? In the middle of so much, I catch a glimpse of you, Rimbaud, and hear your song.

Coachman's anguish. This is what we feel. Rimbaud, your desire is of the plains, and the ages, and all that will come to pass.

A reticence. It is like the morrow that does not fade. It is like you and me, that has the way, and knows the way forward.

Rimbaud, you are at the staging post. You are the life, as we are the need. You are the tomb, as we come across you – yes.

The hollowing of the wood. It's density has a harbour, and the winds of time are your invective, Rimbaud.

Rimbaud – what is this? It is the way we sing, and the way we live, and the way that everything has itself a flame.

'Get a job, by such and such a date, or your out' – that was your mothers invective towards you, and indeed you were out, and off to Paris as a poet!

You flirted with Verlaine in your first letter to him – and you sent poems, which he thought were fine indeed!

The nesting place of all that lives.

What is here now, is fate – sometimes capricious, sometimes steeling, sometimes in awe. Yes that is it!

A special fund was set up for you Rimbaud, to use at your entry into Parisian life. A star was found!

What is left of us? In the nascent alcove, we see all. Much like you Rimbaud, and then some.

The traipsing over hill and dale – we see new life, as it embarks on its lonely journey to places unseen.

The temperature is always fluctuating here, as if the mould of life was not to be as it is. Yes Rimbaud, yes.

What is there to see now that we have left? There is more than ever before, Rimbaud.

The sullied, and the stretch. Be the one who winds, and there will be distance in your steps Rimbaud.

The newness of the fading light. And here, where steps are made for lightness, a new gathering, Rimbaud.

The listening we do, is all about the wandering. And now, where we seek new things to find, there will be happenstance, and the writings of all.

Rimbaud, have you ever listened? Have you ever thought of coming into the night? Yes, I believe it to be so.

The solace of the winter. The solace of the spring. Rimbaud, you are of the fire, and this much suits you.

The gathering of rose petals. There is much to be said, and only a little to be taught. We know the way, it is yours, Rimbaud.

A far reached thing. A thing that does not despise itself. This much we weep, in the tent that is the forest, and the now which is the wind. Rimbaud.

On the day of your departure for Paris, Victor Hugo, returning from his 'fourth exile' stopped at your station to have lunch, but had missed you by an hour!

The saying and the doing. What awaits you Rimbaud, is not the shire, nor the meadow, but the roundabouts and the rest.

When we come to see you, Rimbaud, we come to see our respective solaces. Your life was a trail, and the following too hard for us.

The simplicity of the day. This much is turned in silk, and the semblance of the tenacity is there in you, as in us all.

What have we found? What have we sought? The desire is the duty to uphold the world cannon as it seeks itself in need. You Rimbaud, are the need.

The further we go, the harder it gets. But you Rimbaud are the night. You are the tale that has no telling.

The weather does not bite here – it instead rains in shards. Rimbaud, you are the mighty, as we are the happenstance.

 The fire in the fireplace. The dreams we had as children.
And what we say is not the turn, nor the worst, but the
whole, which is you, Rimbaud.

The sighing of winter blooms. The twilight of the act. What
we feel is never enough. What we have, is enough.
Rimbaud.

The distance in the mire. The only thing that we have to
guide us. Rimbaud you are a tethering that announces itself,
yes.

A garden in the middle of nowhere. A museum whose art is
of the ages. What we say, and what we feel – are they two
different things?

Verlaine, despite your life, you never wrote a bad line.

Rimbaud, your hourglass was full at both ends. Your need,
our need. Your life, our life.

The forest and the sigh. The sea – the sea. The horizon, the
twilight, the clouds, what of them, Rimbaud.

The tether, and the goad. What is more than this? What has
the sun got to say about the shimmering of the sky?
'Rimbaud' – simply.

Your belief is not to be found amongst the winding roads of
temperance. But what of it? Yes, we must live, and here be
ourselves.

The diameter of the play. The shining of the soul. And here, you once again feel, like we all have felt, and know ourselves to be true.

The willows, and the bark. It sheds from every tree that was. Your life is the bark Rimbaud, as ours is from the willow.

We read your life – and we cannot follow.

Coming again, like lightning in a pot of clay. Do not be the spirit, be the test, and you will have all.

A shimmering, we find you. You are still here, Rimbaud, despite all that is written. You are the one who vanishes before our eyes.

Come closer, we wish to see you! Come, come into the light. We will not hurt, but only reconcile the consolation!

Upon your arrival in Paris, you missed Verlaine at the station, and made your way to his house.

The next thing we all knew, it was over. Rimbaud, you are the sand, as we are the tusk.

The difference in velocities between this heart and the next is enough to placate us, Rimbaud.

What have we thought, but everything that is. What have we said, but all. Rimbaud, you are the test, as we are the longitude.

The nearness of a fading sun. And here, where we whisper sweetness to our lives, you will come Rimbaud. You will come.

The further we seek, the less we know. The further we travel, more moisture wells up in us for our tears. Rimbaud, you are here.

The forest is not a vagabond, the earth is not a sphere. And when we see ourselves, Rimbaud, we see the sky as it blooms.

There is here a sometimes quiet calm. But at other times, Rimbaud, as you know, the voice of steel.

When we say things that are in the mist, there is evoked a splendour that does not rise. Rimbaud, do you think so?

And when the troubadours place down their instruments, is this where we seek Rimbaud? Yes, I must say so.

The wishing by the stream. It comes to us in mighty threads, and it knows you Rimbaud to be the spark.

A happening that does not happen. And here, where we believe in so many things, there will be a taste of it, Rimbaud.

The furthest shore. Have we reached it yet, I hope so. And then, a mighty strength comes, which is yours Rimbaud, as it is ours.

Paul Fearne

I am pleased with what I see. But there can only be one way to go. And that is through Rimbaud.

The will and the rite. The solemnity, and the ageless. What is within our grasp is still to be found. Yes Rimbaud.

There is a place, that is no place. That is nowhere. That has no taste. And here Rimbaud, the semblance of all that is.

What have we said, but that which the dreaming relies upon. What have we said, my Rimbaud, that is not unsaid.

The foraging for flames. It is not our task, to be the ones that wander. It is only our task to be, and then find!

The trees in the forest, Rimbaud. What do they say, what have they seen, what is it that holds them upright?

The miniature of the real. The cataclysm of the fire. When rain comes…yes Rimbaud, there will be a might rejoicing.

I see only one thing, and that is the travelling of fireflies to their ancient home. And here, where we sing loudest, a new type of belief.

Rimbaud, do you hear me?

What is there now, but the plateau that weeps. What is there now, but the sheen of treasures unknown. Rimbaud, you are the harvest. We gather you.

The flight of recompense. The solace that the dream pursues. What is next cannot hurt.

The dragon and the storm. The violence of it all. I have heard it said there are no strangers. But what of the flock and the beam?

There is here a saying. Rimbaud, correct me if you have not heard it. It precludes the domain of sense, I will not recount it.

A lying awake. An awareness that lies. And here, where we do that which is for the closing, you will come Rimbaud.

The further we go, the longer is the destination. Your destination is ours Rimbaud.

Gone is the tide. Here is the rush. Rimbaud, you are a sentinel, that does not guide, but which barks a sound unknown.

The truth is in the awning. The solace is where we weep. I have found no other way than this.

The flying of solid things. I do not hurt. I do not weep. I have seen all of it. I have lived all of it. Rimbaud.

The first time I saw you, I was asleep. It was not a dream, but a soporific hallucination. And now, what do you say to that, Rimbaud?

I have felt no other way. I have felt the distance between us. I have felt the wind when it does not rain. I have felt you, Rimbaud.

I have not written a bad line!

And here, where we come for the harvest, there is more than enough to sing about. But, you Rimbaud, you intrigue.

The tethers that do not bind. The strings that do the puppeteering. In this, there is no similitude, but the whole of life, and more.

Rimbaud, your acceptance into the Parisian milieu, was enough to throw you from your life, into the very other.

The niceties of fate are in the wind. It blows hard, but with the sand between our toes, we will prevail.

Having the chance to rescind all, and not taking it. This is where we lye most at the precipice. People come, and people go – but you stay Rimbaud.

I will not look, but when I do, there will be a prevailing wind.

What is in us, is in every one of us. And now, when we have seen things aright, we will not capitulate for anyone, not even you Rimbaud.

The storm, it comes, but we are ready.

What is this? This thing that shimmies through the grass? It is us, as we hold ourselves for something new, and something old.

Rimbaud, are you with us? Are you here? Yes he is. Good. And now we must sing our must ardent song – and we will!

The frost, it bites. The sound, it beckons. What is it that is said – we will never know.

The mist, it comes. It comes before us like a shine that has no hearth. Rimbaud, are you the shine?

Gaining, believing. What is next? Is it the leaves from the vine? Is it all that is in us? What is left? It is you, Rimbaud.

A sitting that has with it the sound of strangers. What is this we wish for? It is the sound of drums, and the barking of leaders.

This is what we say. We say it with a strengthen inflection, and a greater need to have what we say heard. Rimbaud, I will wait.

Having, and wishing. The dime is poised both ways. And here, where we see ourselves to be true, more, or less – yes Rimbaud.

Forgetting in the mist. Forgetting we ever were. Forgetting all that, and then more. Do you forget, Rimbaud?

Having the way opened by the most wicked of adventures. Rimbaud, do you see now? Do you see?

Very much the next, very much the height. Delusion strays, and lifetimes warrant! Have you life, Rimbaud?
The vast expanse. It hovers, and needs no rope to pull it back. Rimbaud, you are the feather that will bring it back.

Grating on our fibrous approach. There is everything, right here, right now, and everything not. Be in tune Rimbaud, we will find you.

The semblance of the chasm. It heeds no address, and no vestige. Be the one who brings, Rimbaud, and you will swelter.

Hanging closely by a wing, the wet will never leave the dry. And you Rimbaud, are everything, and everything despite.

A canopy that is left open, despite the weather – we must feel it, and let itself bury deep within. Yes, Rimbaud, I hear you.

The grain of rice that straddles the infinite divide between what we have now, and what you have Rimbaud.

A fashioning that doesn't leave us. Rimbaud, we must think.

Greeting the maid, and knowing, by her palms, what work is. And that you know Rimbaud.
The sense we have, that the lightning is a wreath. Rimbaud, yours is the withering, the belief and the throw.

What we all aspire towards is the catch in the hay. And here, where we love the night, there will be more to tell of.

What is your way? Mine is the brush and the groom. And in the middle of it all there lies a tightness to end the misunderstandings.

The furrow and the temperance. Rimbaud you have seen what we never could, and your lease is the lease of the daylight.

The harrowing of our ease. There is never enough to shine, but when it does – yes the distance is in the dream.

A fixation to believe. Rimbaud, your hands are not tied, to any thing or any one. And when we see you, we only see your shadow.

The dominion of the world. It is your world, Rimbaud, as ours is the further shore. Come to us then, and see your rupture.

The finding, and the receiving. Rimbaud, you are the cord, as we are the stepping stones. Do not be afraid, there can never be more.

Grating on the silence – the world moves, as you do Rimbaud. The world in all its sense. In all its nuance.

The heaving and the marrow. What have you, Rimbaud? Have you the silk, or the tourniquet? Do you spell? And in what form?

The wretchedness of the weight. It is so hard to carry. And yes, you, Rimbaud, where do you wait? And in which guise?

The seeming, and the rectitude. The seething, and all that is left. Rimbaud, you are the master, as we are the foundlings.

Come and cry a bitter seed. What is more, we will have the light before it is too late. Yes Rimbaud, you mustn't wait. What have we thought, but the merriment. I am the soul, and like the light, I see you Rimbaud and your vast adventure (an adventure that still goes on).

His is the freedom and the need to be. But we are the mass that will never halt. Rimbaud, you have won!

What is this thing? It is you, Rimbaud. What is the laughter we hear, and where is it coming from? It is yours Rimbaud, and it comes from the beyond.

Have we searched enough? Yes we have. What have we found? All that is. And must we begin again? The answer is no.

The trap of the steel. The nuance of the fates. What comes, will only come for you, Rimbaud.

The fire, and the ice. The love and the rectitude. Must we be in tune? Unbearably so. But wait there is more. How much more?...Rimbaud, yes.

The sentience and the noise. What is here, could fill a bastion. But we still linger, for who knows what. Rimbaud, I will come for you.

There is a sound. It is the sound the dawn makes as it falls above the horizon, and touches each of us. This much we know.

What is the making of the scene? Why don't we write about it in a letter, and post it home. This much Rimbaud I will do.

Upon your arrival in Paris, there was a dinner had in your honour!

The seething and the dawn. The hurried footsteps that collide in wonder. Rimbaud, you are the water vapour, as we are these steps.

Bringing with us the fruit. Bringing with us the fruit in labour. Rimbaud, can you guess who we are?

Having our fill, and then releasing the shards. Rimbaud, you are the harper in a harpers land. This much we know.

Saddling our horses, so that we may come through the mist. Rimbaud, where have you come from, and where are you going?

A sound, and then what? A place to be, and a place to have. Rimbaud, where do you hide, so that we cannot see you?

There is more on this plateau than we should hope. But what say you, Rimbaud? What do you hear now that you are alive again?

Juggling this, that and the other. Rimbaud, you are the bleating of the winter solstice as she prepares for one more year.

Catch the glass, before it sees us through. Rimbaud, where are you? Rimbaud, do you have the night and its dew?

Coming in for some weather. Rimbaud, are you the one who sighs? Are you the one who saddles close and hears the spritely fuel?

Changing things, for all the things that have no fear. Rimbaud you are a ghost, as we are the ones who dance.

Do we come close to the fibre of things? Yes, in a round-a-bout fashion. Rimbaud, you are the severing that has no ties.

Rimbaud, why do you not sleep? We all sleep here, but you are still awake. It matters not.

Rimbaud, where is your circumference, where is your moat? I feel it is here to run a fashionable place.

Digging in the pit, we have ourselves found the dire and the retrograde. But here, we come back, and then, discover what we really need.

A forest that has no centre. A castle that will not stand still. And then…more again.

What is this I see before me? It is you, Rimbaud, but you are different. You are the one who shimmers with the age of an old lamp. Yes.

Having the blown wedge that sees only itself. And here, where the night is like a vanquished table, I turn to you Rimbaud.

What is there here, but the semblance of the tide as it washes us out to sea. The beyond. The great beyond.

Gaining in the way of things. You are the heard, Rimbaud, but what of your fate? Do you drink to time to hear her music?

A moistening of the feathers of flight. And when you are strong, Rimbaud, you will come for us like silk, and have your way with so much!

There is now a saying. It says, be the one who harks, and yours will be the tempest and the ghast!

More than is willing!

Have we heard more than is enough? I write these words for you Rimbaud, and only for you.

The match, and the sigh. The withering, and the barking. Rimbaud, you are the key, but we unlock you from yourself.

We do not see you, despite your brilliance. But now we do! And with this comes a solemn rite. The rite of spring.

Holding on, we see the sands of time. And you are here Rimbaud, despite everything that has happened. Yes!

I will come for you when you sleep! And now I must away, to that distant clime that is the hour and the time.

I feel your pleasure. It is the sighing of ancient dreams. Rimbaud, you must not be the one who forgoes, for we are deep.

We weep! And then enunciate the tether! And here, where we are but strangers in a forsaken space, we find you Rimbaud!

What is more, is not less. What is less, is not more. And now, in the meantime – tentacles, and a mash of superlatives.

The test, is in the strength. The way, is in the feather. Be one Rimbaud, not many. Be one, and have your best entailment!

Gaining, riding, being the troupe, and the core. Hearing the milestone as it envelopes all. Rimbaud, you seem unsettled.

Having the freedom, and being what you want. Having the feeling, and going for it. Being in the mud, but sucking for air. Rimbaud.

This is the way of things. There is a tutelage that harbours no doubt. Rimbaud, can you hear the way?

Seeing, and not believing. Hearing, but not in the way we think. There is more than the best of us, right here, Rimbaud.

Do not force the tread, it will only come unstuck. This shoe must take us through many miles. And Rimbaud, you are the one who can say when.

Driving the carriage far. We have not seen this distance in many a hopeful times.

Rimbaud, what of you? Will you come with us, on this journey that has no end? I hope so.

This is not all. We come again in the night, that night that solemnises all. Be the one to fight Rimbaud, I hear your call.

A happenstance that leaves us bending. What we have in the forest of the day is untold in its nomenclature. But Rimbaud, you will come.

A nicety that does not follow. But we all must follow, that is the given and the rush. But Rimbaud, you will never follow, that is your choice.

A landing that contains all. We land on our feet, we feel with our tethers, we are what we are not, and here oblivion.

A great succulence, and then over. Rimbaud your night-time is a right-time – a right-time to be sure. And then, the distance.

A couching in terms. An argument between two friends. I will come for what you are, and then return every last piece of the puzzle we are piecing.

Forgetting, it is a gift. One you never had, my Rimbaud. But in the meantime, a vast array of what is best.

Dreaming. I dream, and then awake. I dream, and then vanquish. Or is that vanish, I can never remember.

In those heady days of Paris, your verse became more regular, your behaviour less.

The boy, the man, what is more, what is less.

The simplicity of things.

The truncheon, and the copse.

Not withstanding.

Having the feeling.

Being right to write.

Coming in for a second glance.

Seeming like it is so.

Rimbaud, you are the whisper that does not sleep. You are the tendrils that bind to no man.

Catch and then release. There is a force here that defies description. And when we are through, Rimbaud – release.

Forests of surging night. Hijinks that require no saviour. Wantings that turn, and dyes that are cast.

Giving more to the dawn. Having the strangest dream. What is more Rimbaud, we will never let go.

A nuance that tenders to no-thing. A fastidious nature that keeps on going, despite.

What we saw in the hourglass, what we felt amongst the trees. It is here! Rimbaud, it is here!

The dimensions of a ship out-weighed. Comingling, aspiring, leading the novice, and keeping his back. Rimbaud – Yes!

What we saw from the deck. It didn't out-weigh us! And then, a mighty crash, and then, you Rimbaud.

The desire to be, and the rocks which form around our combined yearning. This distance does not shape. It only comes for you, Rimbaud.

And then, the task. It weighs as a lightness around the hips. And then, foraging, like never before.

A prefecture, whose lands are not of this world. There is one thing there, and only one thing – and that is art gallery that knows no seeds.

Not knowing which way to go – but we have no map, and our only sense is our sense of touch, Rimbaud.

What is this herald, that harks the breaking of the day? It is us, as we find ourselves once again in the midst of all that is.

A newness, like a breaking of sun on the clouds deep in winter. Rimbaud I have found you, despite the travelling.

The seeming, and the impossible. And when we are there, a new flight into what awaits. Rimbaud, the sound of it.

A grain of sand, it does not linger. It spades in unison with the stars, and has milk as its larger dreaming. Rimbaud, a little longer.

Before the last, a semblance of the ilk. And then, when the timing is right, a missive that does not send, does not send us to brink.

Being scolded. There is nothing that does not tribe. And here, where the gaining of autumn light is amidst, you Rimbaud.

A forthright nature. This is the key. But when we saddle our horses, they will come for us, before it is too late.

The tempest, it is in the way. But we must go through it, before we can say nay. And here Rimbaud, a fortress.

A classic that has always been read. A feeling that has no respite. Rimbaud, you are the glass, as we are the weather.

 What do we see in it? What is there to do, but fade away?
Rimbaud, you are the mist, as we are the seething. Come,
we must away.

A class that does not speak. A forest that only yawns. And
here, here the tendrils lye, a vastness that heralds as it
shines.

Forgiving, but not forgetting. The dew weeps, as we enter
into a vast array of soul. Here we come for you my friend.

Rimbaud, are you the one who speaks? Yes you are. Well
tell me then, what do you see, now that you have entered
the great beyond? I am intrigued.

A closing of fires. What is the time it takes to bend a
sycamore branch? And here, we learn to love, and forget,
we will be true.

Rimbaud, the sense we have is enough to still a raging sea.
But what of the day, as she barks it rapid might? Yes.

A gaining into the night. A Whitsunday deliverance, and all
that shall bear fruit. Here we are not trapped. We see
ourselves in the larger turning.
Drudging through all that is. And now, we gain that most
treasured belief, that thing that does not weep. Rimbaud,
you are here!

The topsy-turvy and the vein. And here, where the night
vanishes from before our unbelieving eyes, we find a new
want, and that is for you Rimbaud.

Paul Fearne

Bringing in the rain. And now, when the sunlight has no stark reminder to give, I search for you Rimbaud, and find you.

Forests that do not budge. A weather that has in store all that is. Rimbaud, you are the want, as I am the deer.

Giving more than is enough. Rimbaud, we come for you before all else. The rain, the rain, the unbelievable rain.

Bringing with us a flagon of wine, we search high and low, and know that the treat will be in the tasting. Rimbaud.

Higher than ever before, the trees dance on solid feet. Rimbaud, be the dawn as I will be the horizon.

A gaining in on things. Your fire is ours Rimbaud. Your fire is ours, and that is enough to test us.

There is no time like the now. The now is the want, as we are the strangers. Rimbaud, you are the jade, as we are the solace.

Be more than is needed. Be the temperance for temperance's sake. And here, where we laugh in greater gusts, a feather, and the rest.

Rimbaud, you seek me. I feel your presence. What am I doing to your legacy? I am fanning it, so that we may both bite.

Rimbaud, a song, if you will. A song to wake us all up. A song to travel down the centuries, and then back again.

A troupe of the unwary. We file through, and know the withering on the vine to be a triplicate of tomorrow. Rimbaud. Gaining in draft. The feathers that let us fly are the same that let us fall. And here, a newness, and a dash of the old. Rimbaud.

Bringing with it all that is. And here, I see you Rimbaud, coming into the light. I see you, and hold you, but cannot let go.

At first light, a fire, something to turn us into gargoyles. And now, I run, run for cover, and have as my scent the dawns edge.

The holding on, and all that will come to pass. And here, Rimbaud, where the sun has set on your life, there is more than the tailor.

Having the dawn, and listening to your call. Rimbaud, was there ever any source to your dealings.

A foot hold, and that is all. Rimbaud, your tune is a lip, and your noise is a solace. Be the charge, and then you will take us.

Grating and seething. Moisture, and then the moon. I am your guide, as you are my solstice, Rimbaud – Rimbaud.

Forging ahead, there is never enough time. There is never enough time. But in you, Rimbaud, the song of the centuries.

A gesticulation. And then the rest. I have never felt more at ease than now. But you, Rimbaud are the sands, as we are the hourglass.

A catching up to the hill. What is left, I hear you ask. Nothing my dear, and that is the wiling of summer suns.

What is here? What is here? Rimbaud, I see you, but you are unseen. I hear your cry, but it is not one of the wind!

A mighty thunder, and then, the crash! Rimbaud, yours is a night without display. Yours is a fathoming that has no want.

Forests that surge with forgetfulness. A hearing that displays no ilk. In the meantime we will come, and see your soul. What is there here, but that which we wish to sanitise. But how can we, when life and the way split and then are re-joined?

There is here a falcon in flight. It dips and wheels in the starry expanse. But what of it, we have nestled closer to strangers.

A gorging on what is left. But here, where we see ourselves in the twilight in a mirror that knows no edges, something else. Yes Rimbaud.

Fly – and have no fear Rimbaud. Yours is the thing that helps us overcome. We read your life, and feel better in our own.

A seeking, and then tomorrow. A seeking, and then life. We have not thought anything of it since we began, but the trouble has found us! Rimbaud.

What is this thing that languishes? It is the world, and we are in it! But that is okay, as long as we have a bow in hand, and a trace to pass the time.

Greeting the waste land. We hold out our hand to shake, and there is no response of any kind. Be the troupe, and they will thank you.

Rimbaud, what is that you see? Do you see what we see? It is in us to believe in nothing else.

Just in time. The fibres of this net have loosened, and we can see our escape. But here, there is nothing to do – back we go to our net!

Rimbaud, have you sensed the way? Can you come for it, in the manner of our choosing? Be the traipsing, and we will guide.

Nothing like it has been seen before. Nothing in its fibres, or its insouciance. And listen, will you, and then we are free to do what we want.

A classless acceptance. What do we find, when the tethers have been unfurled, and the light shimmies. Nothing, but all.

A force – the powers, they have me, but I will it. And here Rimbaud, there is a sense that what is right will never leave us.

Rimbaud, are you alone? Do you seek restitution? I have it that the time is like a lark, and the starling will not peck us.

Surely, we must not wander. Surely we have the distance and the stave. Be the feathering, and yours will be the wet stone.

First, but not foremost. There is a trap we cognise in the depths of night. It is that strange capture that belittles all.

Rimbaud, are there things for the treasuring? Are there things we must not fight against? To be sure.

A god-forsaken ineptitude. And here, we sing like never before. Like never before.

Rimbaud, are you here? Are you in the midst of it? Are you amongst the feathers that have no time?

Catching, and holding. Being, and believing. Watching the sun go down, and then up again, all in the one night!

How many? How far? How long? How, in the middle? How at the death? How in the scheme of things? Rimbaud.

There are times we chase, and times we let go. And here, where the tempest seethes, there is a mass of inconsolable emotion.

Vociferous and unruly. Coming together like sand. What we had in the distance was all that we have wanted.

Come for me like invigoration. Come for the support. The support of what? Not your support, Rimbaud, but ours!

I never thought the wind would be so strong. I never thought the chimes would bleed. But now, there is a fire that has no flame.

A gift, but what is it? A time for shaking wreathes, and unknown deliverances. Rimbaud you are the test, and we have passed.

Grains of ilk. I see my face in yours. Grains of desire, they swim, and are placated. What is there left? Everything, Rimbaud.

A Fahrenheit, and then going slow. We do not see the time, but we feel it's presence.

 Silk, and all that it will bring. Love, and the night. Love, and the day. Love and the light. Love, and yes, it's lack.

What is more amazing than ever, is that we have no sense of what the dye is cast with. And here, a bit of space.

Grating, despite acceptances. Listening despite what is told. And here where we tune our bows to a fever pitch, desire.

 A thing believed in. A rambling that tells a tale. But the distance is like a barrier, that enforces no want.

Rimbaud, there is more. Rimbaud, there is much more. I will find you unto the reaches, and then – hooray!

Come and find a lute, but do not play a merry tune. Put it away, and then come for the revelry of the daylight hours.

Dreaming, but not wanting. Loving, but doing away with.
There is night-time in us already, all we must do is look.

Catching the last of it. Feeling like its predecessor. Rimbaud,
I know you can hear me – Rimbaud?

A fish, that coddles up to the sea. A bird, that has lost its
way home. And in the middle of it, a fading star, that shows
the way.

Horses that no longer need to carry the coach. A whispering
that flies as the wind. And here, a feeling, that has never
been felt before.

The wayward and the settled. What is the difference
between these two songs? It is there timbre, and the
unknown.
Forging ahead, despite it all. Trying again, and again, and
again. The merriment of the stars. We sing for you.

You, you are the sense, as we are the horizon. You come in
reticence, and then in boldness, and then you just come.

A feeling that does not sleep. Rimbaud, there is more to say.
I wish I had time for all that is, but one must away at some
point.

Dreaming – to dream, to sleep, to remember our dreams, or
rather the ones we want. Rimbaud, yes.

Rimbaud, do you feel? I do not, but I have other things to
take my time. Believe in this one thing – fate.

Rimbaud, I see you. I see your suffering. But do not let it be mine. The rainbow knows only silk, but that is kind.

A chance, a rapture, a need, a desire. Where are we? Where are we now? Rimbaud, I sense your presence, but I will not fall.

Bring with you a flagon of water. Bring it quickly. I am on fire, and need to be doused. But do not be afraid, I cannot hurt.

Rimbaud, your dream is of the stars, but what of the rest. There is much to do, and much to say.

Having the station, and feeling its frustration. What can we say, now that the light is of the mire? Do not be afraid.

Rimbaud, there is more here than the rest. But we have rest, when we need it, and know it to be a thing of purity.

The seething, and what comes next. I have found a way, Rimbaud, and it is not yours, but the starkness of the daylight.

Catching a glimpse of all that is. When we are now relieved, we can soldier on, unto the palace of the newness, and the rising sun.
What we thought was an echo, is nothing other than ourselves as we rush for that distant shore that is the hearth of so much.

Gaining the shore, and having it come. But now we see ourselves in that larger breath that is the night and all she is.

A test that knows no strength. A window that looks onto nowhere. And here a blessing that is not of you Rimbaud, but your life.

Forests that harbour no drought. Beings that saddle towards the dawn. What do we say, when the dreams of a thousand nights are upon us? Rimbaud?

Grating, and never restraining. Always finding, but never doing away with. And here, a levity that has no time. Rimbaud

A sky that sees. A never ending round-a-bout. What the day has forgotten is not of us, but of the other, as she turns in silk.

What is this left? The furrow that has no brow, the stepping stone that releases as it ensnares. Rimbaud, do not fight, there will be time.

Fire light, and noisome brigands. What is the high, is also the low. What is the night, is also the day.

Come to the gathering Rimbaud. There is here a light that only shines, and a break of belief that beggars. I will come for the light.

Rimbaud, what do you say? Are you here to fight your way, or dismiss the semblance as a curse? The choice is yours.

Water that has no movement. Sound that has no echo. The feeling of the sea as it barges into one big crescendo.

Sight and sound. Sight, and wound. Wounds that wind. Sights that simplify. And then some.

Rimbaud, the mist is at your door. It does not knock, but lets itself in before your unbelieving eyes.

Do not force. Do not negate. Only wander, from shore to shore, and get a good glimpse of the sea. It is your rite.

Rimbaud, the how, and the why. What we see, in the in-between moments is enough to triangulate a path through the waves.

There is still time. There is still time. Rimbaud, can you hear me from where you are? I come for you, and your legacy.

Mist, and transience. Wandering forth, and back again. Do you wander also Rimbaud, or do you simply wonder?

A silence that contains all. More than enough to hollow out the load. Rimbaud, do you seek, or do you sight the chance?

There is enough in us to feel free. But Rimbaud, are you the prize fighter, or does you flight leave its mark?

Beginning, and then knowing. Having the fireside, and then not relinquishing. Rimbaud, do we see fate?

Receiving the guest, and knowing of his mind. Rimbaud, yours is the foundling, as ours is the repartee.

The gasping, and the well-spring. There are times to shirk, and times to be in the midst. I will be there, despite.

Rimbaud, will you come for me? Will you sail on the sea of dispassion, so that your stave is a thing not seen?

Rimbaud, are you a traveller in whispered night? Are you a sense amongst the nonsense?

Without care, without reason. With splendour, and with help. Rimbaud, you are the need as we are the belief.

Forests that harbour no thought. A treasure that feels itself coming. And in the middle, a change. What is this change? It is us.

I am the one to be, and then not to be. I see you in an intractable light. And then, when thinking is right, a vanishing.

What we always knew, but never let go of. What is this temporal span, that guides as it hushes?

Rimbaud, the sand, it takes us. It takes the very fibres of our being, and has them blown up despite acceptances.

Hounding, and then....There are chances that have no song. There are new needs that have us floundering.

Rimbaud, what do you say? What do you say when all is lost? You say, yes, and then rock the boat that one more time.

Horses that have speed. What do we have, when speed is lacking? We have the clouds as a royal embrace.

Come now, we must not lose heart. There are so many things here that we cannot speak. But still, there is the thrill of it.

Having an eye on the distance. Having what is best, and then, having it again. This is the way to live.

What do you say, Rimbaud, that has not already been said? What have you seen that has not already been seen? Well everything.

Bringing up the rear, and then harking back again. Rimbaud, yours is not the way of temperance, but this is okay!

The catching, and the rye. The need we have to be what we cannot. The need we have to sail to further shores.

What is this? This water that gives no respite? It is the world, as it shimmies back and forth. It is the world, Rimbaud.

Hanging on, but until when? We must hurry, the gates of Hades are closing, but we sneak in for a closer look.

Come and see what I see. It is not for the faint hearted. But you, Rimbaud, have seen it. Yes you have. And now?

Verily, and like a dagger. It is the mist, and I am the incumbent. Be the thing which sways, and all will be yours.

Rimbaud, there is nothing to say. There is nothing to say, only because we cannot see in this gloom and dank.

Closer now, but still far. Closer, but then some. Be the dance, and the dance will carry you. Rimbaud, are you the dance?

There is still enough time, to see the wreck which is the daylight. And here, a solemn oath is said, and all that can be.

The destiny of the stars. Their movement is our movement. Their dreams, ours. And when, Rimbaud, a sound, we will be quiet.

Calamity, and what is now said. The fire that burns, does not burn for us. It burns for all, and in you Rimbaud, we seek larger turnings.

Fickle, and unsaid. Fickle, and more than enough. To transpose the music of the spheres, that is a feat.

Come and be a passenger on this carriage, it will take you far. It will see you miss your station, but then, no more.

Rimbaud, the sense we have is senseless, and the things we are, motionless. But we will come again and again until we are through.

A never-ending ride that only keeps us moving. And here, where we see straight, a motion that only stills us.

Rimbaud, do you see? Do you see, what we have because of you? Yes that is right, we have freedom to be. Yes, it is grand.

What is this thing called hope? Does it just spring, or is there more to it than that? We may never know.

Rimbaud, the dream. Rimbaud the place to be what we want. And here, there is a noise. It is the noise of the dawn on stained glass in a ruined abbey.

Furrowing in on things. Having the wit to say 'I do'. Holding the branches on a hundred trees, as if we never were.

A whistling that brings no respite. And here, where we find ourselves anew, much time is spent renewing old acquaintances, and building new lives.

Rimbaud, do you mean what you say? If you do, then my hat is off to you, and then I am away.

Horses that do not run. A butterfly that can only see. And in seeing, cannot see its own beauty!

Rimbaud, do you run? I know you walk, but do you run? Let us desist, walking is the only thing which matters.

Hovering by the lamp of life, Rimbaud you sing, and in singing, liberate! I bet that wasn't your intention!

In the mist, we draw. We draw on life, on silk, on sand, on the very fibres upon which we walk.

Having the margin, and feeling it's wroth. Being one with the jade of life, and never letting the semblance of ourselves get in the way.

Foraging, and seeing more. There is a cost, but only for the rampart, not for us, as we see again the further shore.

Rimbaud, are you away? I do not see you when you blink. You vanish as if time itself.

A catechism, and then fire. But that is your way, Rimbaud. That is your way. And then…who knows!

Velvet on silk. Transpositions, and transport. What has the carriage got for you Rimbaud? Mist, and song, and wonder.

Grains of nothingness. They seep in here. And when you have had your fill of them, Rimbaud, nothingness, and a damp desire.

 Can we say more? We have to, and then chime our bows for another adventure. And here Rimbaud, flight. No – fight!

A nuance, and then time. It stretches, and out lasts. But in every one of us, the power to outdo time.

Watching the measurements as they are made. Feeling the freedom of a lonely road. Rimbaud, you will come for us.

What is frightful, and inane. They come in equal measure, and know the truth to be a thing that binds.

Forests, and seething trees. Having a window onto the now, and here, seeing it to be the thing that will save us.

Rimbaud, are you a traveller in the night? Do you require a place to rest? It is here for you, if you so desire. Desire and traipsing.

Forging ahead, we cannot believe ourselves. What we have found is more than we could have hoped for. And now this, and that, and all. Rimbaud.

What is this thing, that jabs and spills and froths? It is the world, as it seethes forward into what is next.

Rimbaud, I have not forsaken you. I have come to do a meagre business, and settle all that can be settled.

Within the confines of this grand palace, there exists a time unknown. There exists more of the play, and less of the damp.

Rimbaud, have you seen him? That one that shapes a yellow belly? In this we find ourselves anew, and come for that fallow place.

The higher, the lower, the lower, the higher. And when we dance, we dance with a forward step that rights itself before the end.

And here, where the noise of life is not so much a din as a wake, there can be no going back, for this or for that.

Rimbaud, are you listening? Do you have ears on your back, and sense in your toes? I hope so.

What do we say, when saying is at its ebb? What do we do, when doing is sharp as winter cries?

Rimbaud, are you alive? Are you the one who has cheated death, and live even now?

The life, and your Latin. You were a bright young thing, and knew how to be for your role as a future poet.

Gaining speed, the earth does not stop. It stops for no body, no thing. And the breeze is like a fable that treasures deep and well.

Feeling like a plague. Feeling like a wonder. There is nothing left for us to be, nothing left for us to find.

Rimbaud, do you see the very tops of the buildings? Do they remind you of past deeds?

Having the stain, and knowing its worth. What do we have here, but the grains of sand that herald only day?

Forgiving, and then relating. Forgiving, and then giving. What is the sport of the shire, as it once again placates?

Testing, wavering, knowing not how. This is the lot of us, as we speed towards the tendrils that bind. What is the undiscovered land?

Grating, foaming, having lost. Here we believe once again in things unknown. And when we sleep, what delvings may come?
 A withering that does not concur. Why have we not seen this place before? Why have we come, and why left?

Rimbaud, I sense your need. You need to be here, with us, to revel in your note. Be the climbing, and we will have all.

This temperature is for more than us. This temperature is for the souls to greet, and the moisture to evaporate.

A classic of the wind. It drives us, this wind – it drives both of us, down to the edges of our respective worlds.

 Having settled us, the time it takes to be once more is beyond us. This is it, neither more nor tribulation.

Hoping to be the one who harks, I find myself gone to further shores. And in this, lack, and a modicum of existence, or maybe not even.

What is this now? The raining of shards, and the dead of night. I have felt all in my time, but now the mist is thick. Rimbaud, I am here.

What is there, but time – time between toasts of empty glasses. And here, where the sand never moves, a longing that fades.

Rimbaud, having the twilight, and all that will come to pass. Be the sceptre, and the rod you carry will be a burden no more.

Fashioned to the in-between, and all the splendour of the daylight. Rimbaud, have you seen this place before? I would say so!

Glasses that do not sit right. An itch that has its time in the time of forests. And now, despite everything, we have won – you and I Rimbaud!

Grating on the ceiling. Feathers that do not float. And when we come, we come in strangeness, and all that will be.

A festival of light, a knowing of the daylight. What I say is more than enough to fill any book. Rimbaud, are you really here?

Brandishing the fire like a new found friend. And when we say goodbye, a temperature that does not stand.

Be that as it may, there is still time. Still time to do the things we want. Still time to do away with the past, and all it has been.

Rimbaud, are you the one? The one to take us to a better place? Yes, and here, what dreams may be.

There is nothing in the grindstone. It hints and guesses, and believes itself to be a wanton truth.

And now, and again, the distance we all thought was a dream is now an invective that hurtles through the hours as a train through the mist.

Rimbaud, are you here? Have I seen your face before. This is not a question but a telling that harbours fate as it does distance.

Be the tempest. Be the sport. Be the thing that does not give a newness to all that has gone before.

Believing, and responding. Rimbaud, you are the fixity that glues, the night that relinquishes, and the day that has only fight.

What is left of it? I fear nothing. But what has it given us, but all. When the time it takes exacerbates the fire, there is only one thing to do, and that is hold on.

Rimbaud, where are you now? Where are your sands, as they fall from the cup of temporality? I believe in you, despite.

At the solstice, there is a mighty wind. At the solstice there is more than can be gained. And here Rimbaud, I search for you.

Rimbaud, are you the gatherer? The gatherer of anecdotes? I think you are, and your adventuring is more than takes the cake.

Adventure – this is what this life is all about. Adventure, without it, there is only suffering.

Forging ahead, there is no time left. We must make it to our preferred destination, and then away – not before too long at least.

Enjoyment, that is what you give us Rimbaud, and the alleviation of our own suffering.

The dreariness of the lantern as it winds its way. Rimbaud, you are the dream, as we are those who you encounter.

Floating on to further shores, Rimbaud. You cannot believe yourself. You now have at your disposal all.

The decadence of the trance. The nuances of the homecoming. What is fought for, is not our souls, but our wits, and hearts and minds. Yes, well done.

A Rebours. This was not you, was it, in your Africa, with your austerities. There was no decadence there through which to swim, Rimbaud.

What have we felt, but the travesty of night, the lonely song, and the wayward insistences. This much we know.

Catch me now, I am falling. Catch me Rimbaud, and I will saddle you a great horse, and we will both ride on to great accomplishment.

The closer we are to each other, the further away we become. This is no slide of words, but a new invective upon which we are thrown.

The distance, I see it. I see it on the horizon. I know that we can make the journey. Let us go, see where we end up.

What is there left? Are there assurances from the night that things won't get worse? Rimbaud, destiny is not at odds with us.

The case of the firmament. It leaves us with sore ears, and sorer eyes. But what are we missing? Only you Rimbaud, in life, as in leisure.

A filling of the way station. We hear ourselves here, and know that the time it takes to carry is not enough to placate us. It is *almost worth it*.

Rimbaud – do you now curse the hour of your birth? Do you send flaming shards onto the mass of rectitude? Be that as it may, we have you now. And we read!

Only now do I understand you Rimbaud! You were sent to relieve us of our own foibles. We read of yours, and find a sort of solace. What a theory, I guess!

Rimbaud, are you the one who seeks? Or is that wreaks? I can never be sure which. Whatever one you are, we know your journey as the solemn rite of May.

Catching on to the slope that never bends, I find my way up in the minutest of steps. And in this journey I am free, and know myself not to be plagued.

The hope we had that this was the beginning. It rings true with us, and now that we have taken foot, we speedily advance.

Rearing our heads, it's time to go. We don our gauntlets and our jackets, and here we go. Into the rain, the cold, and the hail. Who feels more alive now?

Rimbaud, are you the one who looks, and then runs, or do you run, and then look. I think I know which. Never mind, life is here to stay.

The harvest has brought great bounty. There is wheat, and every conceivable food stuff – won't you come to eat Rimbaud?

You used to eat out of dustbins to sustain your self – but no more!

Catching the sign of trade, we move forward and have our needs transposed into a higher music. Will you come Rimbaud? Probably not!

What is there sight of here? Is it a deep chasm? Is a graduating meadow? Is it the spring-time over hill and over dale? Maybe. And Maybe we will never know!

Rimbaud, are you still of the streak of distress? Are you still of the vagabond outage? And sometimes we just do!

 The ticket is carved in wood, this much we know. But how long will it last? Until we need it, this much is for sure.

Rimbaud, do we see our respective selves as a flight or as a brawling mass? I would like to avoid it, if it is in any way possible - so let us see.

What we have, is something more. What we have is never anything, but just enough. And here we languish, but not before too long at least. Don't you think Rimbaud?

Hiding in the forest, and not knowing which way to turn. Will we come out Rimbaud, and see you before it ends.

There is more in us than before. More life, and more sound. More of what is good, and what is just – but we must not forget you, Rimbaud, the 'little monster'!

I tug at your shirt sleeves like a child in the daylight. I tug at your hat, and see it fall. But who falls Rimbaud? Or do we all fall?

Wishing to come closer to the edge of acceptances, I read of your life Rimbaud, and know that it could work! And this to each to make our lives that little less onerous.

Hanging on, despite the play of things. I hear you song Rimbaud, and know your fire to be base. But here, oh here, enough!

You make our lives better by seeing the unbelievable adventures you had, and all the things you did. We are placated in our own lives.

Rimbaud, does the constancy of the stars placate you? Does the belief that we all had console you? This much I am sure you must think about.

There is a time worth knowing. It is your time, Rimbaud, as we seek ourselves again in the evening mist. Yes, it is your time.

Rimbaud, do you dream of further shores, ones that have no bite. I think we all do. But that is okay, despite things – yes.

Resonating with the truth, your words were a stepping stone to something greater. But what is this? It is more than all.

Hanging on, despite things. Hanging on, and into the future that awaits. What is this thing – it is our lives, as we hurry this way and that.

Believing what can never be believed in. Forging ahead despite the head. What is more likely – this or that? I say that, and am consoled.

Catching on the seam of things. Having what can only be said to be enough. Rimbaud, you silence me, and I am tethered.

Holding the fort, and then, having it taken. What is this? It is nothing more than the wind of the world, as it scatters us.

Gleaning the mystery as it unfolds. Having a surety that life will present. And here, Rimbaud, a further glimpse of all that should be.

What have we found, but the goad and the night. What have we known, but all that is (with the occasional exception).

Rimbaud, are you the one, the one to take unseemly strength, and have it won? Yes, that is what we thought.

The dressing of old wounds, and wounds that do not stray.
We find a way through, and into, and beyond.

Rimbaud, do you hear me? Do you hear my voice in waves
of night? I hope so, then you can hear me say – 'jump'! And
then, victory!

Fleeting as it is, this life condones itself to far out places.
What have we thought, but more than enough. Yes, and
then through!

Grating, and jarring – your life Rimbaud, that has only the
portentous. Seeing only things through, and then seeing
more besides.

What is this thing that binds us to the raft? It is the littlest of
things, and yet, it is the largest. What is it? What is it? Yes,
and then...

Holding back, and seeing through – are they mutually
exclusive? I think not. I think only in prisms. The refracted
light serves me well.

Henri Fantin-Latour painted a group portrait with you
Rimbaud and Verlaine amongst other poets. You only sat for
one day!

The noise is not a scream. The noise is the same. And here
where we idle, there is a majesty that brings you peace, or is
that in pieces?!

Foraging for what is left. We feel no pain, but there is still
suffering, we feel what is new, and what is benign.

Listening more intently, the merry wives come to put on their show. They will not give up, as neither will I!

This time is for us. This time is for all we have gathered. This time, is for the starling as she brings a bitter harvest.

What have we told, but that which is in the wind. What have we been, but all that rests in the night.

Rimbaud, are you laughing? At whose expense do you laugh? Do you laugh at my expense? I hope so, because it means something true.

Forests and the dream. Forests, and the mightiest dream. There is no larger dream. And this said, now we can rest, and live our lives once again.

A gaining in things that have no harp. A gaining in things that have distillation at their base. What is this we now have – a modicum of respite, and a handful of happiness.

Coming to the closure without care. Coming to the medium without an idea to speak of. This is now the journey, and the homecoming!

Forgetting what we came for, Rimbaud! Forgetting what makes us live! This is the beginning of something more, something less.

Grating, and gnashing, holding, with no steel, we are here, like a foreigner in a strange land, like a troubadour without a lute!

Rimbaud, do you come with me – finally! Do you listen beside me, like a finger before the harp?! Like a mat before the boot?!

The horizon sees me, and is displeased. The moon, the stars, the clouds, all are displeased, but the adventure continues.

Rimbaud, what is this I see? – It is a way to continue, to keep what I have, and still saddle up my horse, and then maybe not!

The brush with the brush of insistences. There is nothing more than this, nothing more than what we have ever thought.

Solid tempests that lay waste. It is futile to attempt a reconciliation, but we must try nevertheless. We must try!

Rimbaud, the sound of your footfall bends us to greater action, and steels us to more of what is possible.

Rimbaud, I laugh with you, in all you heartiness. I even come close to singing with you, but can only find your lowest note.

Is this what we have come too? To lose, and then find ourselves at the end. As I understand things, they are now, and that is all that is here.

Coming close to the harbour, I will have a new need wrapped around, and a folk-some way to clench things with.

Rimbaud, are you gathering the harvest for me? Do you have that strength left? I sincerely thank you for your efforts, they do not go unnoticed!

Forging ahead, despite. There is never anything greater than fate. There is never anything greater Rimbaud, as you have seen.

What do we do to challenge the doors of this vastness? What do we do to make sure we can make it home? Rimbaud, yes.

Catching our ease, as the words from an old traveller, who still seeks, despite what goes on before him.

Flourishing even, despite the cold. Flourishing, and then gaining in surety. This much is known before it is snatched away.

There are traces, in the milk, that leave no hindrance. And here, where time beats in a slow beauty, there are more chances.

Rimbaud, have you come home? Rimbaud, have you sailed in silk? Rimbaud, have you gone against the grain?

There is no capitulation here. And if there is, it is for a larger purpose. We must not sing again, it is written.

What of the blowing of the gale, Rimbaud? Does it impede our progress? No, it only enhances our drive to go harder than before.

You have said to me many times Rimbaud – 'I do not wish to come'. By I implore you again – come, it is a right royal adventure. So you accept!

There is in this mist a chance to really become unencumbered. Do you see it Rimbaud, or do you shirk? No you don't! Excellent!

Forgetting ourselves in steel. And here, where strength is considered a gift, there is more to tell of than can be thought of.

The fight – it is literature. There is no greater thing. No greater fight, don't you agree Rimbaud?

Verlaine asked you to join the fight on your first meeting. And this is what he meant, wasn't it! Yes, good.

What has strength, and subtlety, at the same time? The great fighting machine, and that is us, as we fight nowhere else that in our chosen life domain.

We fight for the dawn. We fight for the sky. We fight for the rain. We fight for our lives. We fight for the moon. We, indeed, fight for the stars.

But most of all, we fight for the need we have to begin once again, and say with solemn resolve, there is time.

A mountain, that has no holes in it. There is only one way passed this bluff, and that is up and over. So onward we go.

There is now a resonating sound starting from the back of my head. It is the sound of you and me as we fumble forward and into life.

Rimbaud, are you still there? Are you listening to this? A great strain has brought me here, but I will bear it (until next time!)

The never before seen gallery. It is here that we find ourselves, amongst the art that has not known the sight of a single aesthete.

The tireless round-a-bout of swings unknown. It is here, where life is in the wind, and sorrow is in the past, that we find ourselves anew, and take a further look.

Rimbaud, you are the test, as we are the rhyme. You are the needing, as we are the default. Be not careful, it is not the way.

Rimbaud, have you found what you are looking for? Have you found what is never at the crossroads? Yes, and more.

There is a difference here. There is more of some things, but less of others. Have we felt what it is to laugh? Yes, and then some.

A grating sound that leaves us perplexed. What have we ever known, but this? What have we ever known, but that?

Having more of the sand, as it squelches between our toes. There is well being here that knowns only time.

Wisps of life, coming in through the window. There is more of it here than ever before.

Vanquishing the cobwebs in our hearts. There is nothing like the now, as it bends us, to write, and have written.

Rimbaud, you are the saving, as we are the life. You are the life, as we are the saving. What does this mean…?

There was once a man, who didn't see clearly. He heard one of your poems read, Rimbaud, and came back from the dead!

What is inside us all. We each have the capacity the reach out, and see the sense for what it is. Do you reach, Rimbaud? Yes, of course.

A great foraging, that has only the meantime as its want. A great need to chase, and all that will come to pass.

Rimbaud, do you saddle up to see? Do you come from that higher ground where seeing is not believing? Maybe so.

A misanthrope to be sure, you had your acquaintances, and you gave your games a mighty rub. Rimbaud.

Having a brush of it. Feeling it stand on us with two feet. And here, there is nothing left but that part of ourselves that will not falter.

There is nothing left, but the task at hand. There is nothing left, but that which is in sight. I will come for you Rimbaud.

The sign on the deck of every ship that has sailed every sea. It says, 'landfall'. And in this there is a truth.

There is nothing beyond this, beyond this place. I am lucky to have experienced this, and I take it to mean a lot.

There is here, a quietude, that doesn't mock, nor does it shine on the grey of cobblestone laneways. It is for us, and all that will come.

Grey, and the darkness of night. Here where sparks define themselves, there is a motion that knows no want. Here, Rimbaud.

Rimbaud, there is a place beyond this place, that has not been seen by any traveller on any sea. It is saved only for the adventurous.

 Telling it like it is. Having the courage to rattle through. Feeling like what is more is less. Gaining in the simplest of things.

Rimbaud, you have a fire that has never burnt so bright. You have a fire that stems from the only things it can, and that is witchery, and the chasm.

Rimbaud, have you found me? I am watching you from the abyss. I have found a way to be here, to watch you unfold.

Claiming the night as our own. I cannot come nearly as close here, but that is okay, for I still see you Rimbaud.

Fastening ourselves to the mast, so that we may hear the sirens song, and not be trapped by it.

This is such an Odyssey we are here in engaged in. There is no greater adventure than that of words, don't you think Rimbaud?

There is a newness in the fjord. It is time to set sail, time for one more mighty adventure!

Rimbaud, do you listen, even now? I think you do. And here, where the brought suffering is at its peak, there will be time for new words, and new ways.

Things that do not rust. And here, where the fibres of a worn out bag dance the new dance of dust, ever motion, and ever steel.

Rimbaud, are you awake? Do you feel as we feel? Do you come to clatter up the wind's sake as it claws itself to the beyond.

Gaining in momentum, are you there Rimbaud? Do you have the signal that we are here?

Watching and waiting, waiting and watching. Is there something more to see here? – It is history as it closes in on fate.

Indebted to the seraphim as she sleeps. She has guided me well. And here, where the mist settles, sleep for me too.

What is more in tune than ever before? What is more in tune than the effervescence of the stars?

A right acceptance that stays only so long as the needs of the dawn. We need them to stay aright.

 A scented page that has no recourse to the real. And in this it lives happily under no weight.

What is more is not weighted with gold. It is weighted with mirth at our expense. But this is not what we are waiting for, is it? We are waiting for the weight to lift!

The new found tide, the tide of a thousand nights labour. And here, we run that arduous run one more time, before it is too late.

Egg-shopping – Shopping for eggs. Do we ever find the perfect one? Yes and no, with more of an emphasis on no! Come and catch a glimpse, you will be surprised!

A further shore – is it a dream? Is it a reality? This much is clear – there is something that guides our actions. Where does this thing come from? The beyond! Yes, but what is that? Perhaps we will never know.

A tell-tale sign that does not set a foot wrong. Boots that are made for the journey. And here, for something else.

The tender hooks of the day. We see past their demise, and into that new thing that awaits, and here, we pull straight up, and away!

Jade and amber, there is no difference. The only difference is in our hearts, and our souls, and our spirits.

Come and be a part of the great adventure, Rimbaud. Even now you can saddle up your horses and come with us – please do!
Rimbaud, are you the one who sees – are you the seer you expected to find? Only a seer can know the way from here, are you now a seer?

Gaining in on the adventure of life. What do we say to it, when it is at its height? We lend an after-thought, and then rattle ourselves.

Couching in terms I do not understand. This is the point of it, to let you see that other place, that is the sentience and the boon.

What is now going to ride? How far? For a very long while. How slow? Very, Very slowly. How much inconsolable? Very Very consolable. This is riding. Riding for strength.

Higher now than we thought, the road up the mountainside takes many weavings and diverging's. We will find our way.

Rimbaud, can you ride with us? I hope you can. Have you even ridden – you haven't. That is oaky, we will take special precautions.

The flat and the out. The motion and the stillness. This is what we want to see! This is what we have come to see.

Rimbaud, and all that is left. What have we come for? – We have come for this! What have we come for? – This!

There is nothing ever even left for us. Rimbaud, does that see a fire start in your gaze? I think it does.

What is life? The life that is left? What is this thing that buzzes and scrapes in the night?

A grain of sand that has no fight. A fight that has no grain of sand. What is the pulse that is left? It is all.

Digging in, despite ourselves. Under the stars tonight. Wishing for you, Rimbaud! Wishing for you!

An agent of passion that has no real sense for the passion of life, nor how it feels to be below the level of life.

Forests seething with forgetfulness. What is now left, is not here, Rimbaud. What is now left.

Dreading what comes next. Feeling the way forward. We see what we see, and here, there is more to come.

Slouching in the presence of someone important. What we know, is enough to save us.

Rimbaud, tether your dragon. Let it's flames besmirch the widow's peak. Let each new urn be a silver to you bow.

Grains of sand that do not stall. Grains of sand that only believe themselves to be true once a year – the mighty round!

Rimbaud, we are testing the waters. We are seeing what is left in the mud and the dirt, and the glaze.

Rimbaud, are you the one to slowly decline? Are you the one who measures with your nose? It matters not – come.

Diminishing, returning, having hope, seeing the difference. What is more, we will have no fear.

Is this in line with the life? Have I transgressed the tenor? To have transgressed then, is not transgression at all.

What is new, is not new at all. What is flat, is not flat. The world is an oyster, which is not flat. See me now.

Rimbaud, are you the toy in the storm? Are you the tethering point that harks back on things to come?

Rimbaud, do you see us now, do you see the life we have led? It is all that we have known.

Streams, and gurgling brooks. Wastelands, and fathomless abysses. What have we been told, but all.

Forging ahead, and not knowing why. Having the fortitude, and then the strength, and then all that ever was.

Rimbaud, are you awake? Do you see the time? Do you know the distance traversed?

Hurricanes and silence. What we find in the middle. What we have no notion of, until now.

Having, and believing. What we thought was a mist, is nothing other than the horizon.

Rimbaud, are you still alive? Have you lost faith in yourself? If not, then come, and come quickly.

What is there left of us? We are a shell, that once had the tributaries of life at call. Be that as it may, we will come.

Gaining in strength, we hear the trumpet's call, and know it to be a thing that will guide.

Rimbaud, are you the one who will take us? Take us to that place that has no fear, nor want of things.

Further in the in-between of things, there is a sound. It is the sound of the dawn's light as it passes through the stained glass of ruined abbey.

What is there now? Now that we have pulled the curse away from our eyes? Rimbaud, tell me about this curse? Was it you? Ha!

Let us say, Rimbaud, that it was you! I have no doubt it was some endearing prank, sent to gather the webs of a thousand spiders.

Fashioning what is left of our ease. You Rimbaud, are the one to tell us a tale of all that is, and then some.

What is the adventurous Rimbaud? You know as much as anyone. Your life was replete with it, that is for sure.

Having the steel to continue. Only you could, yes. And then, what we say when we laugh.

The strength is what we have, and here, where the music always fades, a new way to be, Rimbaud.

Rimbaud, the test is in the water, as the lark is in the way. Come now, do not be shy, we will only follow you.

To be the waters. To see their clarity, and to feel their rub. What is left of us? What is left of us?

Rimbaud, are you the temptation to part? Are you the unwholesome that lies in every one of us?

Having the need return. What is in faith an extract of the un-nerved, is nothing other than the wheel of a giant.

Rimbaud, do you come in lightning shifts? Do you spasm on the breaking of the day? Is this what we can hope from you?

Rimbaud, your life consoles us – at least I am not that! This is your way, and your want.

Having the fire, and not being burnt. This is what you have given us, when we read your life.

Paul Fearne

Clouds that do not see. A sky that only awakens. And here, where we love with passion, there is passion for you Rimbaud.

A great symphony in an unknown forest. This is where we cannot go, but that is fine.

What is this life? But the wing and the need. What is this life, but the changing of every guard in the night.

There is a time, Rimbaud, in the distant future, where everything will be settled. And here, we will come.

Noisome, and in acceptance, we litter forward, and are consoled. Rimbaud, are you the one to take us there?

Having the wandering of fireflies. Here we look back no more, and only in the distance do we see.

Rimbaud, do you change your countenance? Do you change it for us? This is like a shark swimming, in the dark of night.

Rimbaud, are you wont to travel? Travel once again to that far away vantage that is the distance?

There is never anything more here to see. There is only the trap and the core, and the newness of a fading light.

Three trumpet blasts – myself, you Rimbaud, and the night. And as there is nothing more to say, I will say it – nothing.

Things spread, and things unsaid. And now, in the meantime, much to do, and much to be in charge of.

Giving way, Rimbaud, there is now time to relinquish. And then, in the midst of it, a new dance to replace the old.

Having new attire. Giving the grip. Sorting forth unto strips unknown. What do we say to this Rimbaud?

Needing nothing new. Heading less. What is the vanity of the stars? To be looked on with fawning.

Gouging the way. Having the fruit, and letting it ripen. Do I come for the semblance of things – I do!

What can we say, when there is nothing left to say? What is most said is nothing other than Aaahhh!

Rimbaud, do we talk in reams of maiden silk? Yes we do, only because fire is the way, as love is the dance.

Why do we have our hats off? It is to guard further from the sun that shines within. And here, there is more to do! Rimbaud, are you the clear sky that follows no ilk? Are you the train that pulls into the station?

Rimbaud, do you bleed like the rest of us? Do you have a point where enough is enough?

Following, and desiring. Meeting far afield. What can be said of this, as we come to another impasse?

Paul Fearne

Rimbaud, you seem to be calm here. But what is that, other than the moisture of your tears.

Catching the time, as if it was a thing to be caught. And then, when the fire in your eyes burns brightest, a visage!

What do we say, Rimbaud, when the night belittles the day? We say more than enough, and then some!

Gripping on tight. Holding on, till there is no more. What do we say, when our flames are fanned?

Forgetting, and then being reminded! Having the stallions of bitterness at your beck and call.

Is there something more to it? Rimbaud, can you see the way? I have not forgotten you, not yet.

Having the standard bearer call the changes. What is left of us, we do not know, but we will try, that is for certain.

Hearing something new, that is nothing other than something old. Rimbaud, will you come?

Finishing the act, and knowing it to be good. What is there to say, when all that is left is a wishing well without coins.

Rimbaud, are you the one to take us to feather-top, and then back again? Yes, we hope.

For what purpose do the sounds of the hourglass come? For what purpose do we feel their wake?

116

What is there here? There is more than can be said. There is in this space a vagabond dreaming, and the all or nothing.

Catching a glimpse, Rimbaud. Catching a glimpse of all that is. And here, a feather – it contains all.

Faith, and the tempest. Here we find ourselves anew, and know that in the meantime, a dreaming that awakes.

Rimbaud, do you hear? Do you drive away the cobwebs, and then have them settled?

What is more than this? To sense on the one hand the proclivities of fate, and on the other, life.

There can never be more than this. This is all there is. Are we sad, are we mad, are we there?

Rimbaud, I test you, but do not find you wanting. I hear your cry, but know it to be a thing of great splendour.

What is this now? A forward motion that does not sleep. A backwards motion that only sleeps.

There is a love that is grander than the moon. There is more to us than we think. Do you agree, Rimbaud?

What has this life given us, Rimbaud? It is not in the eye to see, nor the earth to believe.

Having the whites of our eyes. There is fear here, but also something different. There is still more to understand.

What do we have in store for ourselves? What do we know that can take us further – further than ever before.

Inching closer, but closer to what? We do not know, and cannot say. But do not lose hope, there is more of it.

Flowers, and silk, and snow, and dreams. These are the things that take us there, to that misty place that has no hearth, but heart!

A gathering – a gathering of the word. It speaks to us, and lets us dream, until what is left is cast in bronze.

The task is at hand, the treasure is in the yoke. And here Rimbaud, a mighty exhale, and then…

What we thought was the end, is only the beginning. What we thought was our strife is our guardian, don't you agree, Rimbaud?

I see you in the covered light Rimbaud. I see what it is that makes you work. I see what it is, Rimbaud.

Crashing down – I know what it is that keeps you. Coming again, I love, and am placated.

Rimbaud, are you the one? Are you the one to come riding on your stallion at the end of the world?

Much that has no silk. A roughness that transpires. And here, a wealth of laurel wreathes, to guide us home.

Rimbaud, do you stay? Do you stay at the rooms that have no fear? I believe you must.

There is only time here. Time, and the acquiescence of judgement. But what have we got, but all that is.

The wisps of winter wind. The blaze of summer heat. Are you the one to send us there Rimbaud?

There can be no more of this, this stern and reasoning drive. We must let go, and then find ourselves.

The distance of the flame. The passion of the heat. And here, one long last look. And then…

Raging, and then the fire. It burns down to its base, and then we are free of it. Coming and going.

Happening all around us, and in us only cold. I see more than the day, I sense all that is.

Looking for the season – is it winter yet? Looking for the season – is it here yet? Looking for the season…

Rimbaud, do you drive us to that faraway place, that is ourselves? Do you see us? Yes and no.

Catching on to what lies next. There will be more time than ever! Be a retrograde for a retrograde son.

There comes a course, that is not for the faint at heart.
There comes a course, that is for us, and not for them.

Rimbaud, do you quiver? Do you quiver at heart when we do not see? You are still here, well your life is, at any rate.

This is now, and this is weak. There is a weakness now Rimbaud that we haven't seen for a thousand years. We have just overcome it.

Planting the shadows like they do not weep. Of course they weep, they weep for us, and for us only.

Ask only this. Ask only, should we fall, or should we float? I will leave the answer to you, Rimbaud.

There is something more to be said. And that is this. The mountain is only as high as the sum of its parts!

Rimbaud, do you steel yourself for the ascent? Do you have the courage to fall if required?

What is there still, and still embracing? It is hearts and minds, and all that shall be. Rimbaud?

The feather and the grind. The wet and the dry. Which will you be, when all is said and done?

A great gust. Do we still allow it? Do we still feel for it? It is here, within us, to do all we can.

What is more than this? Is it the sharp and edged? Is it the
raining and the nom de plume?

Having the strength, and seeing it come forth. Do we fear it?
Yes and no. We see it sometimes, but that is fine, Rimbaud?

Forests that surge with forgetfulness. A bird that remembers
the way home. A nest that has the fibre of tenacity.

What is it here? It is the life we lead, but never thought
would transpire. There is something more!

There was once a newness, but it has faded. There was
once a chance, but it is here now. Rimbaud, do you see?

Gathering up the mist like an abandoned alley. Seeing
strangers in the in-between of things.

Rimbaud, do you feel? I do not, but that is not what is at
issue here. What is at issue is the raining of the clouds – will
there be a flood?

Greetings from the margin of things, Rimbaud. Greetings
from all who have ventured far to come to this place.

Have we set our hearts a-beat that one more time? Have we
sent our ships through to distant shores?

A gaining that has no rhythm. A gliding that follows the path
before. What have we here Rimbaud? What have we here?

A distant wreck. We swim out to it, and climb on it. There is nothing that it cannot be, this wreck.

Rimbaud, do you see? Do you see this wreck that lies basking in the sun? It is for us, and for us only.

What can be seen from this height? What can be known about the land below? There are chances that do not fade.

Rimbaud, are you listening? Are you there to listen? I suspect yes, and no. Yes for the spade, and no for the heart.

Having the steel to continue. What have we thought, but the neverness of time. And what have we been, but the fullness of the adventure?

Come now, I beseech you. Come to this place Rimbaud. It is a magical place that does not let the sand in.

There are niceties that do not hold. There are things that do not drudge. But here we see ourselves anew, and know time to be a carrier.

Having more than we thought. Rimbaud – do you see yourself? Are you there before us?

The catching of the rain. It does not stop. It stops only for us. And here, we say yes, and forget ourselves in wonder.

The repository of hope. Indeed, there is a chance to be everything I want to be, and then sing like no other.

Gaining into things. Having the rainbow, and knowing how to look at it. Being placated, and not knowing why.

Rimbaud, are you sane? Rimbaud, do you travel to places unseen? Yes you are, and yes you do.

What is the furthest you have travelled Rimbaud? How did you get to Africa, might I ask?

Having the temperament to really go that extra mile. But what of you Rimbaud? Have you been?

What is it that keeps us here? What is it that keeps the ball rolling? Is it you, Rimbaud, and I? Yes.

Rimbaud, do you set sail on the wind? Have you ever seen the back of the blackberry bush?

Clawing, and catching, writhing and whittling. There are two signs here, we will take the high one!

Testing the way. Is it right for us, this journey? YES!

Can we believe in ourselves once more – do we have that faith? The trees will say yes.

Rimbaud, do you tender fashioning silks unto the rush and the warbling bird? You must.

Is there more time here than equated by the dance? Do we see unto the firmament that travels with no heels on its shoes?

Is the solstice a yearning, and the dream a letting be? I will go for it, and have the sense to be alleviated by time.

There is a feeling that no doctor can dispel. It is the feeling of you and me, Rimbaud, as if we were children on the sun kissed shore.

Have the rectitude to be. Have the silence not to undo. Be that what it may, we have no sense for the senseless.

What is this now, a blankness the envelopes? I see you fold, but know not what you have in store.

Come for me, oh one! Come for the silence, and stay for the laughter. Rimbaud, you are dancing on lighter steps.

Zeroing in on fate. There is a chance that the vapours of the night will only carry me as far as I want to go – well no, in fact!

Have the treadmill, and your turn will only come. Have the silence, and the choice will be yours.

Rimbaud, are you waiting for us? Are you waiting for the truth of it? Come now, do not be afraid, we will come.

There is nary a shore that does not speak. There is nary a bird that does not keep. But here, all of it.

Rimbaud, do you speak? Do you speak of deeper things? Yes, your depth is the depth of the night.

Come now, do not be afraid. There is nothing that can hold us back. Nothing that can be, and then, not be.

What is this thing that bites? – it is the world as it shimmies back and forth. Are you still here, Rimbaud?

There is a place, that resides in every heart. It is strength and persistence, and timely adventures.

When we are there, rest and recompense. Until then, onwards we go, with staff in hand.

Having the need to be what we must surely be. And then, a little bit of respite, and all that can be.

Rimbaud, do you see me? Do you see the covers as they move ahead? Then be, and rest a while.

Rimbaud, are you in sight? Are you the one who lingers by the door? I will see you again, not before too long.

White on black. Shoes filled with sand. Can we agree on one thing? It doesn't matter.

What thee, clouds about? Disseminations with the throng. Are you the tether, maestro?

Saving in the hedge, being true to the gondola on appease. Have you found what you are looking for Rimbaud?

Fighting the sense we have to be senseless. Rimbaud, can you see me? Can you see the fibres of the day?

Having the margins fold in, having them be like we were, (and that is now!) and come, we must not linger.

Grating, and seething, having the way forward seen. Must you appease the ferryman, before it is too late?

Drumming, and tuning. Being the one who smirks, are you the window unto our souls. Wait there is more.

A fish, and the cake. Do we eat more than this? Do we eat our fill on the smell of things to come?

Rimbaud, are you tired? I am not, and that is not final though. I wish to be that thing that laughs.

And here we sing! And here we laugh! Rimbaud, are you the one to travel to more distant lands? Of course.

Is this the one we seek? Is this the one who bellows? We know more than ever before.

Having the strength. Having what is important. Having the need and the want. Rimbaud, I will find you!

Is this the thing we seek? Hands on hands. Dirty through the dimension. This is it, my friends!

Jilting and then forgetting. Being the one more stable. Have we got the might? – I think we might.

What is here, despite the chasm? We see above it, and
know it to be a charm – illusory, and not impeding.

Can there be a time more likely than this? We must not
wander – but when we do, we wander with sheer brilliance,
Rimbaud.

Have we got ourselves right? Are we the ones to tarry?
There can only be one outcome, that is true.

Rimbaud, are the mists with us, or against us? Does there
seem more from their movement than meets the eye?

A gathering that has substance. Rimbaud, do you bleed?
Are you human? I think you are more than human!

What is the point of this? What more can we say? There is
something more, and it will shock – there is here nothing.

Giving in to the night. Finding more of a chasm than a clan.
Being in touch, so that you Rimbaud, can have your way.

There is a touch of unease about the whole thing. Rimbaud,
do you see the venom from the mulch. Here, a peculiarity.

What is this that does not encounter? Is it the stallion and
the vault – the timely reminder, and the leaving it be – never!

Forever bleating, forever estranged. Forever new to the
motion of the stars. What have we got, Rimbaud, but all.

The guest, and the wonder. What is next? That is not a question we should ask ourselves!

Rimbaud, do we need more of your motion through these lands, or can we suffice without them?

Wishing, and wanting, having the course of the riverbed. Rimbaud, are you the treasure?

Coming back to it, we have had so much to tell of. I once rode a horse, and it nearly bucked me.

Rimbaud, do you see your venom, even now. Despite all that has been written about you, do you see it?!

A masthead that leads the ship astray. An encapsulation that has no errors. What are we to do?

Rimbaud, are you well? Have you gone now, to your home and recompense? What adventures await?

Fastening onto the raft, we see down, and see ourselves. What is there left, Rimbaud? Nothing.

The water runs quickly, but we run even quicker, Rimbaud. And here where we wait, an avalanche that pushes us deep.

What are these arches? Why are they made of sandstone? It is an ancient university, where there are no students.

A climbing we all do to stave off the night. But what is the night, Rimbaud? Is it a friend or foe? That is for each of us to decide.

Having the laughter, and doing what we will. Being in tune with so much, and not letting on.

A jump into the dark that sends a shudder. Be quiet, I beseech thee. There is no time for noise here.

Dreaming of, and dreaming in – what is the difference, one of semantics I hear you say.

Forging ahead, you are made of steel Rimbaud. Your life is a receptacle of so much, but only because we will it!

Feeling like a wind that doesn't sleep. Having the shutters down to find a way. Rimbaud, are you the one?

Holding all aloft. We celebrate, without accoutrements, but with souls full of mirth. This is how it is.

Do you not see, old friend, are your eyes closed, or are you just blind to the world? This much we must all be, if we wish to travel.

Grating, and restraining. There are larger things here, larger than we had hoped. Be with us oh great one!

Hiking into the wilderness, we follow. But where we leave off is another question. We will ride.

I come for you, oh night! I come for the adventure of it all. I come to be the one who gives, and gives rightly.

Be the sustenance of an age. We drink, and are not consumed. We tarry, and believe once again that life will take us.

Come to me, the dreaming and the sorrow. I will raise you up and have your branches cast in bronze.

The need, and the desire. What we thought were our ashes, are nothing other than our wings!

Rimbaud, do you test? Do you test us with your lack? We all lack, but yours is a mighty keepsake.

Jade and armour. Armour and silk. Which of these do we need, on this, our final journey?

Fire, and the treading. We tread on the flames, and put them out, but what is left, but all?

Dragging, and staying. Staying, and dragging. What do we do Rimbaud, but defy the day, and all she has.

Your depth lingers. But what of your intellect? It knows only one way, and that is up and through.

Kindness, does it rest on you? I am not sure. But we will feel it if it is there. Rimbaud, you can tread.

A youthful lodge. It doesn't matter now, it has shaped me, and made me into what I am.

Rimbaud – the fire, the range, the rooftops and the bear. What is this we say with you – a heard cry.

Having the sense to be. Having the sense to right the ship, and have it sail on calmer waters.

Rimbaud, do you accost no one? Do you see the way to be again? All you do leads up to this.

There is a light – it is buried deep. It shines, but we do not see its rays. We must dig deep, and lo! - it is found.

Tightening the grip. Seeing that little bit further. What do we say, when we come across it? Yes!

Joining the fray. Having the courage. We will not settle until we are done. Rimbaud, do you see?!

What is left, is more than nothing. What is left equates to the sand. We hear you Rimbaud, and then some!

Walking in the likeness of a swan. And here, we suddenly find ourselves. Not believing, only remembering.

Rimbaud, do you fathom each walk you did? Are they there with you now? I should hope so.

Youth, and age. The designs of fate. Are we there? Have we come to the station without a ticket?

Rimbaud, yours is the way of the pen. Yours is the way of the pendulum. Yours is the way of the strike.

The mist beckons. We must intuit which way to go. We must be on guard, this much is true.

What has always been, has always been. What is new, has never broached a net, or maybe it has – let us see.

Sands, and the hourglass. What is wanting is only tiresome. What we can find, that is what we live for Rimbaud.

Rimbaud, there is no more to say! You are a genius in a strange guise, and you perplex us, but you are great!

But indeed, one thing more, I must say. Your cry, why is it unheard? But we do hear it, but we must listen so intently, and in the right places, otherwise we are deaf to it. We must be in the right mood, have the right lighting, have your books about us – and then, and only then – epiphany!